PRAISE FOR
AI PREVAILS

"James Simpson has written a riveting, whirlwind tour through the promise and danger of uncontrolled development of technology. From genomics and nanotechnology to superintelligence and radical humanoidization, the noted economist and Senior Fellow at the Foley Institute writes lucidly about how AI and robotics are radically changing how humans relate to each other and the world around us. Simpson explains the intertwining roles of science, wealth, and government leading to the frenzied race to technologize, and the consequences that have not yet been fully considered. Calmly assessing the risks and benefits of new technologies, the author avoids doomsday theorizing and makes a major contribution in suggesting the "precautionary principle" as a guide to future development. *AI Prevails* is a sobering but measured exploration of the scientific ambitions, dreams, and nightmares shaping our lives in the future. The analysis is at once chilling and hopeful, a must-read for anyone asking the fundamental question: *What should our future look like?*"

—Cornell W. Clayton, C.O. Johnson Distinguished Professor of Political Science, and Director of the Thomas S. Foley Institute for Public Service and Public Policy at Washington State University

"It is true that life has become more comfortable with technology. But, as Professor Simpson meticulously spells out, ultra-rapid development of robots and artificial intelligence (AI) is a sign of a new era, an uncharted zone for humans. Unlike authors that specialize in the future, the author is careful to avoid doomsday theorizing. Uniquely, he presents facts based on his economic and scientific background in a way that makes an engaging and hard-to-put-down read. Professor Simpson has an unparalleled convincing case for a practical method to deal with research on superintelligence and the specter of joblessness. That is the European created internationally used legal procedure termed the Precautionary Principle to protect humankind by seeking to proactively regulate risks. Rightly, and with vigor, he argues forcibly against the United States regulator's approach for evidence of actual harm before regulating. Not only is that in violation of international law, common sense tells us to avoid a situation we will regret in the near future."

—Masaru Yamada, freelance journalist

"Simpson's portrayal of our planet's plausible future just a few decades from now is a wake-up call for humanity. Moral, ethical, theological, and political ramifications of artificial intelligence must be addressed now in order to ensure a safe, fulfilling life for our children and grandchildren. A fascinating depiction of robotic and humanoid development that reads like science fiction—and sure to engender lively discussion for your book club."

—Bernice Konkell, entrepreneur

Inside Robotics

Poverty Bay Books

Book design and publishing management: Bryan Tomasovich, The Publishing World
Author photo: Masaru Yamada

Simpson, James R.
Inside Robotics: Robots and Humanoids, Now and in the Future

ISBN: 979-8-370-23285-5

Also for sale in ebook format.

1. Computers / Artificial Intelligence. 2. Computers / Intelligence (AI) & Semantics. 3. Technology & Engineering / Robotics. 4. Social Science / Future Studies

Poverty Bay Books

Distributed by Ingram

Printed in the U.S.A.

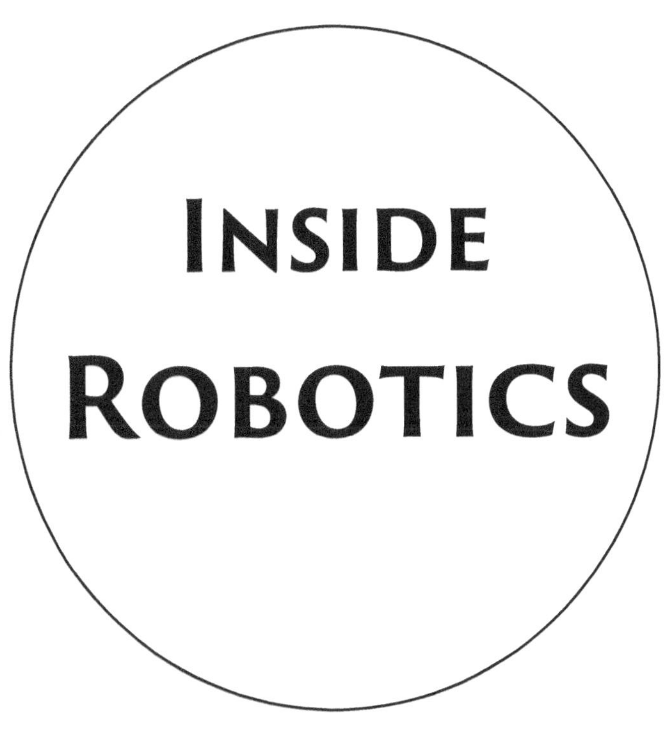

Robots and Humanoids
Now and in the Future

JAMES R. SIMPSON

Introduction

Years ago, it became evident that robots were taking jobs from blue-collar workers. I then realized these robotic technologies were being thrust upon an unwitting public. It became clear to me that the natural trajectory of this movement was toward advanced robotics. That was when I decided to take on the task of writing about what is behind such developments. During my science-backed research as an economist, I became curious, and then passionate about uncovering what it would take to place controls on robotics just at bans are argued about on superintelligence.

Researchers all over the world are racing to develop technologies using robotics. We have all seen sci-fi movies focused on robots. Developers in robotics, the branch of technology that deals with the design, construction, operation, and application of robots, are endowing humanoids with extraordinary features. Within a few decades they could be on par with or even exceed humans. If not contained, repercussions could be drastic, like the creation of a new species that could evolve from mixing humans with humanoids. My concern is about scientists and others who believe they have unfettered freedom to develop any technologies they desire—regardless of consequences to humankind.

One of my main objectives in this book is to provide something for everyone thirsting for more knowledge about humanoid creation and development and to make the content informative for people at all levels of scientific knowledge on the topic and simultaneously a pleasure to read. I know readers of this book vary from those with minimal interest in how humanoids will be developed, to those in the multitude of scientific fields who have a deep interest in certain aspects of the innovations and creations. To that end, I encourage both types of readers to enjoy critical thinking about how the humanoid timetable might change and especially the building blocks for humanoids.

PART I

THE REALITY: ROBOT AND HUMANOID NUMBERS GROWING FAST

We live in a society exquisitely dependent on science and technology, in which hardly anyone knows anything about science and technology. This is a clear prescription for disaster.

—Carl Sagan, *The Skeptical Inquirer* (Volume 14-3, Spring 1990)

As expected, there are complications in robotics development. Technology developers might make it possible to build a robot more intelligent than any human. If the enhanced robot breaks away from its creators, it could then potentially even write its own source code. Critical question. Will we control robotics builders, or will they control us? What would it mean to be human in an age of enhanced robots and humanoids that will coexist with, or replace us? Should we citizens simply internalize a life of uncontrolled robotics in which the technologists have *freedom of power* to do as they please?

The question of gaining happiness from any kind of robotics developments is an intriguing one. Could such an event truly happen in our lifetimes? Will developers of robotics control us, or will we control them? So, could, would, those robots and humanoids be happier than when they were not enhanced or were mildly enhanced? Would their lives be more meaningful and enjoyed than if they were not enhanced?

How about humanoids? Some of those creatures can be on par with humans by the mid to later 2030s. By my prognostications, mildly advanced humanoids with truly humanlike features and characteristics will begin to fill positions once taken by humans in 2035. Five years later, in 2040, significantly advanced humanoids as living creatures are likely to be on par with humans. Sometime in the following five years, some humanoids will have capacities that exceed those of humans if there are no regulations or bans. Radically enhanced ones could feasibly make choices that might result in a new species' being created

Does that bother you? So, in reality, what can be done by the citizens to assure appropriate measures are taken, at prudent, well-judged times, to avoid catastrophes resulting from radical humanoid development? If the populace is concerned, should citizens fight back, But how? In fact, as citizens, do we even genuinely want to be in control of our lives?

Definitions

Robotics is a branch of artificial intelligence that deals with robots. Let's pause for a moment to define a few terms to help visualize the role of robots, humanoid robots, and humanoids in our not-too-distant future. There is no consensus on what constitutes a robot, even in the field of robotics. A general description is a mechanical or artificial device guided primarily by a computer program or some electronic method. The easiest explanation has been *you know one when you see one*. At least you could—until a few years ago. Now, in our supercharged technological world, the term *robot* includes all sorts of programs and mechanical and digital devices.

Popularly, the terms *humanoid robots* and *humanoids* share the same definition: a robot based on the general structure of a human that has an appearance resembling that of a human being. Confusingly, an *android*, widely written about and starring in movies and TV programs, is also a humanoid robot designed to look and act as much as possible like a real person. Equally bewildering, the terms apply to both sexes, although technically, androids are the male form and females are *gynoids* (a.k.a. *fembots*). The terms *bio-android* and *android* are interchangeable. *Droid*, a robot in science fiction, is an abridgement of both android terms.

The use of the term *humanoid*, rather than *android* or *humanoid robot*, has been an attempt to humanize the mechanical being and make it more acceptable, even lovable, in daily life. The stumbling block is that there is no black-and-white distinction between a humanoid robot and a humanoid. However, that difference will become increasingly perceivable as humanoid robots gain humanlike features, begin to mix with humans, and have rudimentary professional jobs. *Humanoid* is the term used apart from robots in this book as a catchall for humanoid robot and humanoid, unless otherwise denoted. At some point, you will know a true humanoid when you see one.

Somehow, the notion of humanoid robots and humanoids as part of home life among the general populace strains the imagination, despite the new reality of the rush to buy smart devices and robotic toys. However, in Japan at SoftBank, robots are family. SoftBank has updated Pepper into a genuine humanoid robot companion that communicates "in an intuitive way, through its body movements and its voice." It can be individualized to offer content by downloading software applications that, based on your voice, the expression on your face, your body movements, and the words you use, can interpret your mood and emotions.[1]

An example of how robotics is engaging the whole family and the workplace is AVA, a 2018 *chatbot*, which is a computer program that simulates human conversation through voice commands or text chats or both. Paradoxically, the COVID-19 epidemic has resulted in numerous technical and social innovations, one of which is that closed offices keeping workers locked up at home has resulted in their turning to PayPal for their purchases. The explosion in demand has led to the use of chatbots for communication; the medium had reached a record 65% of message-based customer inquiries by late April of 2020.

Additionally, there are *cobots*, or co-robots (from collaborative robots) that are intended to physically interact with humans in a shared workspace. Offices, college campuses, and other locations in numerous countries have leaped, in a matter of just two years, to using food delivery services by robots. In a new twist, a Chinese girl bought a robot that mimicked her handwriting, enabling her to avoid the tedious repetitive homework involved in learning Chinese characters.[2]

However, there are social drawbacks, for "a new wave of automation could also mean that when companies start hiring again, they do so in smaller numbers. 'This may be one of those situations when automation does substantially depress

---

1   "Pepper, the humanoid robot," AdAstra, 2020, https://sk.adastragrp. com/en/healthcare/pepper/#:~:text=Pepperismuchmorethan,adaptsits- behaviortothem.

2   Daniel Victor and Tiffany May, "Chinese Girl Finds a Way Out of Tedious Homework: Make a Robot Do It," *New York Times*, February 21, 2019.

rehiring,'" said Mark Muro, a senior fellow at the Brookings Institution who studies labor markets.[3] Companies and other enterprises that seek to reduce costs will increasingly engage humanoids.

---

3   Michael Corkery and David Gelles, "Robots Welcome to Take Over, as Pandemic Accelerates Automation," *New York Times*, April 10, 2020, https://www.nytimes.com/2020/04/10/business/coronavirus-work-place-automation.html.

Robots and Humanoid Robots, Creation to the Present

Let's shift gears again. The public is aware of and informed about fictional robots and androids. However, few people realize that the origins of today's robots date back over two thousand years, during which time only slight modifications have been made.[4] These fictionalized automatons are a regular occurrence in the works of Homer, Plato, and other classical authors. *The Leizi* described the first automaton in the vicinity of 250 BCE. Around 50 CE, the Greek mathematician Hero of Alexandra described a machine that automatically pours wine for party guests.

In 1206, Al-Jazari described a band made up of humanoid automata that, according to Charles B. Fowler, performed "more than fifty facial and body actions during each musical selection."[5] An elephant clock that incorporated an automatic humanoid robot mahout (a person who works with, rides, and tends an elephant) struck a cymbal on the half-hour. Leonardo da Vinci designed a humanoid automaton (a self-operated machine) that looked like an armored knight in 1495.

About 100 years ago, Karel Čapek was credited with coining the term *robot* in *R.U.R. (Rossum's Universal Robots)* in 1921. After that, there came an exponential explosion of interest in robots that continues unabated in its growth today. The first robot put to useful work was named Televox and was created by Westinghouse in 1926. The Westinghouse Corporation

---

4   The list of fictional robots and androids is huge, occupying 30 printed pages in Wikipedia: see "List of fictional robots and androids," accessed November 4, 2020, https://en.wikipedia.org/wiki/List_of_fictional_robots_and_androids.

5   Charles B. Fowler, "The Museum of Music: A History of Mechanical Instruments," *Music Educators Journal* 54, no. 2 (October 1967): 45-49.

then created a humanoid robot known as Elektro in the 1930s. Elektro was on exhibition in the 1939 and 1940 World's Fairs. In the 1950s, George Devol and Joseph F. Engelberger started Unimation, the world's first robot manufacturing company. The first industrial robot was Ultimate, which worked on a General Motors assembly line in 1961.

Robots and androids have spawned a gold rush in the form of books, movies, and television shows thanks to people's intense fascination with these fictional and real creatures. Fritz Lang's film *Metropolis* depicted gynoid robots called Parody, Futura, and Robotrix in 1927. In the 1930s and 1940s, Isaac Asimov published short stories on robots. His first novel, *Pebble in the Sky*, was published in 1950. His short story collection called *I, Robot* came out the same year. The *Foundation* series was first published in 1951 and continued on into the 1980s. Jack Williamson picked up on that theme and published *The Humanoids* in two novels, published in 1949 and 1980 respectively.

Science fiction (a.k.a. sci-fi) took off in 1950 with *Roman*, a robot bent on destroying the earth. There were even radio series in the 1970s and 1980s that featured robots, such as Marvin the Paranoid Android in *The Hitchhiker's Guide to the Galaxy* BBC radio series (1978–1980). Tidy, George, Fagor, Surgeon General Kraken, and miscellaneous other androids were featured in James Follett's *Earthsearch* BBC radio series that ran 1980–1981. "Accident-prone and apologetic gopher robots" were featured on the BBC radio series *Nineteen Ninety-Four* in 1985. *The Digital Human* on BBC Radio had its last episode in March 2018.[6]

The film *The Clever Dummy* played in 1917, when the term "robot" did not yet exist. Television films and series began with *The Adventures of Superman* (1952–1958) and "The Runaway Robot" episode (1953).[7] The number of comic books, graphic novels, comic strips, web series, and video games is impressive and growing, thanks to animation.

It has taken a relatively long time for robots to globally make significant inroads in industry, the service sector, and

---

6   Wikipedia, s.v. "List of fictional robots and androids," accessed November 4, 2020, https://en.wikipedia.org/wiki/List_of_fictional_robots_and_androids.

7   Ibid.

agriculture. There were just 55,000 industry robots worldwide in 2002. That was the beginning of a torrent of innovation and realization about the value of robots. The number leaped to 2.4 million in 2018, and 3.8 million units are projected for 2021. Continuous rapid growth is forecast.[8]

---

8   The International Federation of Robotics, 2018, https://ifr.org/downloads/press2018/Executive_Summary_WR_2018_Industrial_Robots.pdf.

Development of Humanoid Robots, and Humanoids in the Modern Era

Creation of humanoids, as we now know them, that have humanlike features, began on a robot platform. Waseda University in Japan initiated the WABOT project in 1967, completing it in 1972 with WABOT-1, the world's first full-scale, humanoid, intelligent robot. It took Waseda University twelve years to finish Wabot-2 in 1984. The outcome was stunning: a humanoid robot musician able to "converse with a person, read a normal musical score with its 'eye' and play tunes of average difficulty on an electronic organ."[9] Six years later, in 1990, Tad McGeer showed that a biped mechanical structure with knees could walk passively down a sloping surface. Waseda University then developed, in 1997, Hadaly-2, a humanoid robot that interacted with humans both verbally and physically.

Development of humanoids began to accelerate at an exponential rate in the year 2000, when Honda created its eleventh Bipedal Humanoid Robot that was able to run. In 2005, Mitsubishi Heavy Industries released Wakamaru, a Japanese domestic robot "primarily intended to provide companionship to the elderly and people with disabilities."[10] NASA and General Motors finalized Robonaut 2, a very advanced humanoid robot, in 2010. That robot had the distinction of being part of the payload in the successful launch of space shuttle *Discovery* on February 24, 2011.

---

9   "Robot Plays the Organ, Next He Will Rip Your Arms Off," Synthtopia, October 29, 2000, https://www.synthtopia.com/content/2009/10/29/robot-plays/.

10   "Robot news," Robotnews, April 6, 2007, https://robotnews.wordpress.com/2007/04/06/wakamaru/.

Singapore's Nanyang Technological University released Nadine in 2015. This socially intelligent humanoid robot is a realistic-looking gynoid who is friendly and greets you in response to your greeting. She makes eye contact and remembers all of the conversations you've had with her. That same year, Hanson Robotics in Hong Kong released a humanoid robot named Sophia, designed to look like Audrey Hepburn. That creation was updated as a social robot in 2018. Since then, much more has taken place in the robotics field that is genuinely startling.

Prognostications on Humanoid Robot and Humanoid Development

I have divided humanoid development into three stages that merge into each other: humanoid robot, advanced, and radically enhanced. To gain a reasonable idea of what may come or is likely to come in the future, visualize the growing up of a child born in 2015 (Table 1).

Table 1: Timelines of humanoid development compared with the age of a child born in 2015.

2015		Child born.
2025	10	First humanoid robots begin to mingle with humans.
2030	15	Moderately augmented humanoid robots begin to mix with humans and hold rudimentary professional jobs.
2035	20	Early advanced humanoids with truly humanlike features and characteristics begin to fill positions once taken by humans.
2040	25	Significantly advanced humanoids as living creatures are on par with humans.
2045	30	A period of radical enhancement takes place around 2040–2045, during which some humanoids have capacities exceeding those of humans.

Now a conundrum. The term *radically enhanced humanoids* refer to those in an extremely advanced stage of development or beyond. They have such advanced capacities that they exceed those of present humans. If there are no bans or controls on humanoid development by the time these living creatures are on par with humans, at that time some would no longer be unambiguously humanlike by our current standards. Some, particularly if programmed with free will, might have the capacity to make choices that would adversely impact humankind to such an extent that a new species might be created. The result would be a posthumanoid condition.

There is, however, an alternative to these dire scenarios. If people have discerned by the mid-2030s there is an existential risk (a risk that cannot be undone and that poses permanent, large, negative consequences to humanity), there would be sufficient time to begin monitoring humanoid development. Then strict controls and bans would have to be placed on further development before 2040, when living creatures are on par with humans. A child born in 2010 would be 30 years old at that time.

It is crucial to understand that the global nature of robotics activity makes enforcing bans and controls very difficult. My dates in the prognostications are not fixed. However, they are not speculations. Neither are they predictions of what will happen, because the events depend on economic conditions, the interest of robotics creators, their funding, profits to developers, and societal acceptance of service robots and humanoids in white-collar jobs. A natural question is on what timeline are these prognostications based. A succinct answer is that I have extensive references from my in-depth research beginning a half-dozen years ago.

Human and Robotic Workforce

The number of researchers who are directly or indirectly involved in technology development worldwide that is related in some way to robots and humanoids is overwhelming. In brief, thousands of individual and collaborative activities are taking place in numerous scientific fields that contribute directly or indirectly to humanoid development. Literally hundreds of thousands of scientists just in America, and hundreds of thousands more worldwide, are engaged in some aspect of fields related in some way to robot and humanoid, even if peripherally.

The IFR reported on the total number of professional service robots, with occupations in fields that include public relations, medical operations, and assistance to the elderly and people with disabilities. This grouping rose 85 percent between 2016 and 2017. The projections are for 21 percent annual growth through 2021. Prognostications of growth farther out for robots, humanoid robots, and true humanoids are hard to make. The best one can say is that growth will increase "a lot." However, one thing is for sure: the invasion of industrial robots will escalate, and service robots will grow early on at an exponential pace. The reason is I am confident that scientists and developers will be intrigued by the challenges because of their great, almost overpowering, desire to create and their love for creating new things.

Finally, be aware that I do not attempt to provide a complete diagnostic of all the technological aspects in the creation of humanoids in this book, because so many diverse fields are involved and new material becomes available every day. What I *do* provide are my well-reasoned explanations and conclusions grounded in my economic and scientific background.

It is important to understand that humanoid development is not just on the drawing board; rather, it is in the humanoid robot stage. Many of the techniques and technologies are already well advanced beyond the current attributes now found in robot humanoids. Detailed information and projections of times when developers might imbue humanoids with further attributes designed to make them look and act as much like a real person as possible are found in:

PART II

BUILDING BLOCKS FOR HUMANOIDS

Man–computer symbiosis is an expected development in cooperative interaction between men and electronic computers. It will involve very close coupling between the human and the electronic members of the partnership.

—J. C. R. Licklider, IRE Transactions on Human Factors in Electronics (March 1960)

My objective in developing building blocks for humanoids is to provide something for everyone thirsting for more knowledge about humanoid creation and development, to make the content informative for people at all levels of scientific knowledge on the topic and simultaneously a pleasure to read. I know readers of this book vary from those with minimal interest in how humanoids will be developed, to those in the multitude of scientific fields who have a deep interest in certain aspects of the innovations and creations. To that end, I encourage both types of readers to enjoy critical thinking about two key topics: how the humanoid timetable might change and at what point humanoids could become an existential risk, and whether radically enhanced humanoids should be controlled or banned—and if so, when and how. There are two sections:

Section I: The Path to Humanoid Robot And
Humanoid Development
    Close Coupling of Humans and Machines
    Mobility, Vision, and Appearance of Robots
    Body Parts Regeneration via 3-D Printing
    Speech and Power to Operate
    Transplants of Body Parts
    Reproduction: Womb Transfer and Surrogate Babies
    Embryo Transfer

Also helpful is the glossary, which contains 150 definitions of techniques, technologies, and other supporting material.

Development of functional humanoids as near equals to humans is rapidly advancing. Example: evidence suggests that robotized humanoids will have sufficient mobility to interact with humans, if the creators want them to, in the not-too-distant future. A team of Harvard University researchers announced the revolutionary first autonomous, soft, untethered, and 3-D printed hybrid between an octopus-like creature and a robot in mid-2016. Each of the functional components required—fuel storage, power, and actuation—is included in "these curious creatures, [which] can perform incredible feats of strength and dexterity with no internal skeleton." This squishy creature is cheap to print and could pave the way for a new generation of such machines.[11] It goes without saying that this innovation can speed up the race to develop advanced humanoids. Now onward to my favorite topic: symbiosis, perhaps because it is an opportunity to tell the tale of my dog Sam.

---

11   Leah Burrows, "The first autonomous, entirely soft robot," *Harvard Gazette,* http://news.harvard.edu/gazette/story/2016/08/the-first-auton-omous-entirely-soft-robot/

Close Coupling of
Humans and Machines

The field of biology is where we obtain background to evaluate pathways into and through symbiosis to creations beyond single-celled, or unicellular, organisms, the smallest contiguous unit of life. [12] Organisms can grow, respond to stimuli, reproduce, and, through evolution, adapt to their environment in successive generations. The 1879 definition of symbiosis by Heinrich Anton de Bary as the living together of unlike organisms now includes all species. Another commonly used definition of symbiosis is simply the close and often long-term interaction between two or more biological species.

There are multiple ways to categorize symbiosis. For the sake of brevity, I will address only one of those systems. Symbiosis can be viewed as being on a continuum between antagonistic and cooperative symbiotic relationships. *Antagonistic* relationships occur between hosts and parasites or pathogens. In the antagonistic relationship of parasitism, the parasite generally gains, while the host is harmed. *Cooperative* relationships are on the opposite end of the spectrum. One such cooperative relationship is known as *mutualism*. Mutualism is where the two parties both benefit. *Commensalism* still lies on the cooperative side of the symbiosis spectrum, but a bit farther away from the end than mutualism. Commensalism, a biological term that describes the relationship between two living organisms where one benefits and the other is not significantly harmed or helped,

---

12   I do hope that biologists do not take umbrage for my impinging on their purview in symbiosis. I am well aware of journals such as *Symbiosis* published by Springer and other sources. The objective in this chapter is to at least add to work, ideas, and interests of others on this topic, one that I take very seriously.

is an important concept in the future evolution of mutualism between humans and machines.

For example, in commensalism transportation by one organism of another or living together in housing is a type of symbiosis. Another is known as *phoresy*, "a type of biological hitch-hiking" whereby transportation is provided by one organism to a second organism.[13] A third example is two organisms living together in shared housing, or one organism taking up residence in the abandoned dwelling of another. It is basically a one-sided symbiosis. Commensalism is an important concept in the future evolution of mutualistic symbiosis between humans and machines.

Some organisms are *obligate*, meaning they depend on another for survival. Others are termed *facultative*, meaning they can live with another organism, but do not have to. Another vital distinction is the classification by physical attachment. Those that have bodily union are termed *conjunctive*, while those in which there is not a union are *disjunctive*.

A common contemporary dictionary definition of mutualism is the relationship between two different living creatures that live close together and depend on each other in particular ways, each getting benefits from the other. The relationships in mutualism may be either obligate for both species, obligate for one but facultative for the other, or facultative for both. Biologists generally have focused on organisms that are extremely or relatively small. However, the term also applies to mutualisms between creatures that are relatively large, such as the goby fish, and those that are smaller, such as the shrimp. These two creatures sometimes live together; the blind shrimp digs the hole, and the fish alerts it when there is danger so it can re-enter the hole. Most land plants and land ecosystems rely on mutualisms between the plants.

From a strictly biological perspective of mutualism, the relationship between humans and machines at present is not a symbiotic one. However, the increasingly close working relationships between humans and robots is symbiotic within the popular definition of symbiosis as a relationship between people, companies, and so forth that is to the advantage of

---

13 Encyclopedia.com, s.v. "Commensalism," accessed September 17, 2020, https://www.encyclopedia.com/science-and-technology/biol-ogy-and-genetics.

both. That is the meaning Licklider had in mind in his 1960 publication about man-computer symbiosis.[14]

The use of words and terms is continually changing. For our purposes, think about *cobots*, robots in a factory that work side by side with humans on specified tasks. That interaction is a symbiotic relationship between humans and machines. Thus, a newer use of the term mutualism is warranted in the symbiotic development of humanoids to mean the way two entities, one human and the other a machine, exist in a relationship in which individuals benefit from the interaction of humans and machines—and even some joining of the two.

The obsession with animal ownership in America provides an example of symbiotic mutualism. In this case, there are two distinct living species involved. Let me personalize a case that many readers can relate to. It exemplifies the condition in which many biologists restrict the definition of symbiosis to close mutual relationships and, in general, only to lifelong interactions involving close physical and biochemical contact.

I got Sam in Tucson as a puppy when I was discharged from the Navy in 1961. We were inseparable. He waited under my pickup while I was in college attending classes, went up with me on ranches where I worked as a cowboy, and was a great asset in dating. Initially, our relationship was facultative. Then, at some point, while my outward feelings remained facultative, Sam's relationship had changed to obligate, meaning he depended on me for survival.

At the end of my study for my master's degree, I began an international career and left Sam with my folks on their farm. One day, in faraway Paraguay, I received a letter saying that my parents' veterinarian had diagnosed Sam as dying of loneliness for me. Unknowingly, my facultative relationship had developed to the point where I felt obligated to send for him. I did so, and he recovered quickly. I did have to leave him with my folks in later years, but he remained in good condition and my visits were sufficient for him to be happy right to the end.

---

14   J. C. R. Licklider, "Man-Computer Symbiosis," in *IRE Transactions on Human Factors in Electronics,* vol. HFE-1, no. 1 (March 1960): 4-11.

Mobility, Vision, and Appearance of Robots

Enhancing mobility in robots is a step in the symbiotic process of adding human attributes to robotic platforms. *Biorobotics*, in the AI field, takes inspiration from biological principles to design robots with mobility that approaches that of animals. The breathtaking cyborgization of humans (a *cyborg* is a complex organism that has advanced abilities resulting from augmentations and enhancements, particularly mechanical parts) is ample to demonstrate that developments in robot mobility have been dramatic. For example, although arms are relatively easy and inexpensive to create, legs are very expensive and complex because of mathematical issues related to adjusting a foot in a certain manner, or even leaning on a leg. However, robots are on the cusp of being able to climb stairs, and, given rapid advances in technology, it is inevitable that robots will have to adroitly get in and out of vehicles.

Now, about vision: the biggest challenge for robots is to make sense of all the data coming into their cameras, because they are clumsy. However, a technology to attach tiny lenses to a sheet of some flexible underlay, developed at the University of Wisconsin–Madison, alleviates that problem. These micro lenses, each about as big as the head of a pin, could, for example, cover a robot's head or body. Apart from mobility, robots that can see are a key to self-driving cars, projected to be in use in the early 2020s. They are likely to be used in a wide variety of industries; for example, food manufacturers combine AI software and advances in laser vision for tasks like slicing meats. The sensing and imaging market will grow dramatically to meet unfathomable demand as devices that mimic vision become even more varied and able to meet almost every need.

Computer makers have now used Intel's computer vision technology, dubbed RealSense, in devices such as laptops and tablets. Intel RealSense technology is a suite of "depth and tracking technologies designed to give machines and devices depth perception capabilities" that will enable them to "see" and understand the world. Intel RealSense technology is made of Vision Processors, Depth and Tracking Modules, and Depth Cameras. In practice, this technology allows users to scan objects and people in three dimensions and put an image in a computer game or to 3-D print a miniature model.[15]

These techniques also permit control of vending machines with a wave of a hand, and, with digital mirrors, allow people to try on clothes virtually. Lowly toothbrushes can now be delivered to hotel rooms by computer vision robots. Paris-based Blue Frog Robotics SAS has included computer vision so that "Buddy, a home robot with cartoonish eyes," can recognize family members in the kitchen.[16]

Much more advanced, and one vital step in the shadowy race to develop advanced humanoids, Intel's RealSense computer vision technology frees up robots to "leave their stationary posts in factories and navigate the real world."[17] By 2016, a grocery billionaire had developed a symbiotic automation system that includes "autonomous robots that can travel untethered among storage racks in a distribution center."[18] In just two years, these robots have become the norm in Amazon and other companies' warehouses.[19] On the individual level, the RealSense technology can also guide

---

15   Wikipedia, s.v. "Intel RealSense," last updated August 20, 2020, https://en.wikipedia.org/wiki/Intel_RealSense.

16   Jack Nicas, "Why Your Gadgets Can Now 'See' in 3-D," *Wall Street Journal*, updated October 15, 2015, https://www.wsj.com/articles/more-devices-gain-3-d-vision-1444859629#:~:text=Parisbased-BlueFrogRobotics,aBlueFrogexecutiveestimated.

17   Ibid.

18   Robbie Whelan, "Fully Autonomous Robots: The Warehouse Workers of the Near Future," *Wall Street Journal*, September 20, 2016, http://www.wsj.com/articles/fully-autonomous-robots-the-warehouse-workers-of-the-near-future-1474383024.

19   Angel Gonzales, "Hands, Heads, Robots," *Seattle Times*, April 9, 2016, http://www.seattletimes.com/business/amazon/at-amazon-warehouses-humans-and-robots-are-in-sync/?utm_source=twitter&utm_medium=social&utm_campaign=article_left_1.1.

customers to the plumbing section of a hardware store. Alas, there goes another job for humankind.

Deep learning technology, which is a statistical technique that enables computers to learn by processing huge amounts of data, has been one of the hottest investment targets for global tech giants for a half decade. One beneficial way to apply learning techniques for machines is by teaching them to recognize spoken words. Research is focused on a kind of self-study program for machines in which computers learn by themselves how to achieve a task, rather than be programmed solely with fixed rules. By 2015, the Japanese robot maker Fanuc Corp. had strengthened a tie-up with Preferred Networks, an artificial-intelligence venture, as part of its effort to develop industrial machines that can learn and repair themselves.

Another physical biotech example is creation of artificial human skin that the recipient will not reject, which has long been a goal in medically oriented research, especially for burn patients with chronic wounds. A positive side benefit is that this technology aids in taking the place of animals in testing products such as cosmetics. Ongoing research is directed toward development of waterproof and flexible qualities like a wide range of realistic skin tones and fully functional hair follicles and sweat glands akin to those of normal skin. Artificial skin has been developed that "acts like it knows when it is being touched and sends out the news as if by telegraph."[20]

An immediate use of artificial human skin is in prostheses. A biotech goal is creation of a flexible electronic covering that, when connected to the body's nervous system, approximates the powers of real skin. It is obvious that these skin technologies will be of great benefit to humans. Examples abound of other innovations, such as "an invisible film," developed by scientists in 2016, "that can be painted on your skin and give it the elasticity of youth."[21] By 2017, developers reported they had "genetically modified stem cells to grow skin that they successfully grafted

---

20   Daniel Akst, "Artificial Skin That Knows When It Gets Touched," *Wall Street Journal*, October 22, 2015, http://www.wsj.com/articles/artificial-skin-that-knows-when-it-gets-touched-1445532088.

21   Gina Kolata, "'Second Skin' May Reduce Wrinkles, Eyebags, Scientists Say," *New York Times*, May 9, 2016, https://www.nytimes.com/2016/05/10/health/second-skin-aging-wrinkles.html.

over nearly all of a child's body."[22] One implication is that apart from making wrinkles disappear on humans, we can speculate that advanced humanoid sex workers and their customers might benefit.

22 Ariana Eunjung Cha, "Genetically modified skin grown from stem cells saved a 7-year-old boy's life," *Denver Post*, November 8, 2017, http://www.denverpost.com/2017/11/08/gene-therapy-stem-cells-skin-saves-boy/.

Body Parts Regeneration by 3-D Printing

Although perfection is in the future, "printing" using the building blocks of human biomaterial is well underway in multiple laboratories to create tissues of kidneys as well as of livers, with the latter being the most regenerative organ in the body. In 2018, Organovo, a company based in San Diego, developed a bioprinting process that takes cells from the patient or adult stem cells and turns them into printable bio-ink. From that, they "build up small sections of liver tissue" by layering biomaterial in "carefully calculated designs."[23]

Many experts do caution that "convincing the government of the safety and efficacy of implanting bioprinted tissues into people" is "one of the biggest challenges" for the industry. Nevertheless, as reporter Steve Johnson wrote, "Despite challenges, many people are encouraged by the impact 3-D printing is already having on health care, especially in robotic prosthetics. There are a lot of hurdles, but there is a lot that shows it is worth going forward."[24]

In an unusual twist on 3-D printing, although most efforts are concentrated on improving the quality of life of living people scientists have developed a way to benefit the dead. The first procedure, announced in 2018, involved initially scanning

---

23 Hasan Chowdhury, "Liver success holds promise of 3D organ printing," *Financial Times*, March 4, 2018, https://www.ft.com/content/67e3ab88-f56f-11e7-a4c9-bbdefa4f210b.

24 Steve Johnson, "Researchers aim to push 3D printing into living organs, tissue," *Seattle Times*, February 8, 2015, http://seattletimes.com/html/businesstechnology/2025649409_3dprintbodypartsxml.html.

the donor's face, in this case a person who was brain-dead.[25] The next part of the procedure was to remove the donor's face and attach it to the living person, a disfigured man. The last step was to attach the lifelike 3-D replica, taken from the scan, to the dead donor.

Naturally, not everyone will volunteer to be a donor for such a procedure. For that reason, the medical community of surgeons and related scientists is continually excited about the next opportunity for unusual innovations—in this case, using a printed face. That conclusion reasonably leads to the question of how long it will be until human body parts are printed for humanoids. And speaking of that, how about using wiggly things to power humanoids?

---

25   Andy Newman and Marc Santora, "For the Living, a Donated Face. For the Dead, a Lifelike Replacement," *New York Times*, January 5, 2018, https://www.nytimes.com/2018/01/05/nyregion/face-transplant-3-d-printed-mask-donor-nyu.html?register=google.

SPEECH AND
POWER TO OPERATE

Humanoid robots and humanoids, like humans, must have power to operate. Several options can be thought up, such as electrical plug-ins for a battery designed for humanoids, much like for electric cars or tools, or filling up at a fuel station. However, sources like that can be bulky and inconvenient, and they don't fit the bill for a humanoid to be on par with humans. Food that is specifically developed for humanoid robots would be a desirable source, so 3-D printers have been developed by such companies as ChefJetPro and Foodini to print out "successive layers of edible material" intended to match ingredients in recipes.[26] That sounds fine. However, food for power brings a problem: waste elimination. This time, 3-D printers become an essential component in a technology to help solve both the power and excretory process issues.

The startling innovation of a 3-D printed hybrid between an octopus-like creature and a robot, with functional components including fuel storage, power, and actuation[27] was created by Harvard researchers in 2016. That feat was added to, in 2019, by researchers at Harvard and Cal Tech. The 3-D printed Rollbot, which can move and change shape in response to external stimuli such as temperature and light, is "paving the way for fully untethered, soft robots" that could lead the way to such robots' being used in medicine and industrial

---

26   Michelle Lock, "3-D printing aims to rewrite the script on cooking and tech," Phys.org, February 11, 2015, http://phys.org/news/2015-02-d-aims-rewrite-script-cooking.html.

27   Leah Burrows, "The first autonomous, entirely soft robot," *Harvard Gazette*, August 24, 2016, http://news.harvard.edu/gazette/story/2016/08/the-first-autonomous-entirely-soft-robot/.

engineering. [28] It doesn't take much imagination to visualize eager developers creating humanoid robots with state-of-the-art mobility and powered by these creations. It goes without saying that this innovation can speed up the race to develop advanced humanoids.

Now on to speech. Our voices are one of our main communication tools, so natural talk is an essential attribute for humans to assist humans in discerning whether humanoids are on a par with them. In 2011, IBM's Watson competed on *Jeopardy!* against legendary champions Ken Jennings and Brad Rutter, and Watson won one million dollars! In 2016, researchers using the International Business Machines Corporation's Watson analytics system developed speech that seemed "very much like a normal conversation with a human being."[29] Apple introduced Seri, the first modern vertical assistant, a short time later. Amazon's Alexa followed in 2014.

Alexa first appeared in the UK and Germany, followed by India, in October of 2017. Teams of linguists, speech scientists, developers, and engineers worked together on Amazon's Alexa to use a blend of Hindi and English, which "she" "speaks with an unmistakably Indian accent."[30] Then, in 2018, Alexa, Siri, Cortina, Google Assistant, and other talking assistants, termed *chatbots*, began to support multiple apps, including messaging apps. [31] The crux of the matter is that we can expect normal conversation from humanoid robots by around 2025, when the first basic ones begin to mingle with humans.

Voice-controlled virtual assistants such as the Amazon Echo, and an increasing number of customer-care websites, are

---

28   Leah Burrows, SEAS Communications, "Self-folding 'Rollbot' paves the way for fully untethered soft robots," August 21, 2019, https://wyss.harvard.edu/self-folding-rollbot-paves-the-way-for-fully-untethered-soft-robots.

29   Melissa Korn, "Imagine Discovering that Your Teaching Assistant Really Is a Robot," *Wall Street Journal*, May 6, 2016, http://www.wsj.com/articles/if-your-teacher-sounds-like-a-robot-you-might-be-on-to-something-1462546621.

30   Saritha Rai, "Amazon Teaches Alexa to Speak Hinglish. Apple's Siri Is Next," *Bloomberg News*, October 30, 2017, https://www.bloomberg.com/news/articles/2017-10-30/amazon-teaches-alexa-to-speak-hinglish-apple-s-siri-is-next.

31   Alexandra Samuel, "What I Learned From Building My Own Chatbot," *Wall Street Journal*, April 29, 2018, https://www.wsj.com/articles/what-i-learned-from-building-my-own-chatbot-1525053780.

the latest signs that big technology companies believe our future involves talking to computers that can talk back. Paradoxically, because the voices sound almost human, a debate is on about whether, at a bare minimum, a bot should self-identify and answer truthfully when asked if it is a bot. However, this issue is insignificant to AI developers who consider speech to be one of the formidable challenges for the world knowledge problem. To them, endowing AI with mastery of aspects of conversation natural to humans like irony, ambiguity, sarcasm, laughter, and puns, is the foremost goal.

By 2018, some scientists were asking whether deep learning is really so deep after all, because there is no real intelligence there—just brute-force algorithms based on huge quantities of data. The problem is that although the software can instantly identify millions of words, heightening interest in using deep learning techniques for speech, there is another way. In 2018, the Allen Institute in Seattle reported it "would invest $125 million over three years in research to generate common-sense knowledge" in an initiative called Project Alexandra. Not to be outdone, in the same year, the Pentagon proposed a five-year, high-risk project with total funding of $60 million on the same topic. [32]

The world's top research labs are rapidly improving computers' ability to understand and respond to natural language. Machines are getting better at analyzing documents, finding information, answering questions, and generating language of their own. The Allen Institute for Artificial Intelligence unveiled a system termed Aristo, for Aristotle, in September 2019. An eighth-grade science level test was passed comfortably, and Aristo answered 80 percent of the questions on the twelfth-grade exam correctly. [33]

One priority software automatically analyzes documents inside law firms, hospitals, banks, and other businesses. In response to this, Jeremy Howard, founder of Fast.ai, an independent lab based in San Francisco, said: "Each time we

---

32   Steve Lohr, "Is There a Smarter Path to Artificial Intelligence? Some Experts Hope So," *New York Times*, June 20, 2018, https://www.nytimes.com/2018/06/20/technology/deep-learning-artificial-intelligence.html.

33   Cade Metz, "A Breakthrough for AI Technology: Passing an 8th-Grade Science Test," *Seattle Times*, September 4, 2019, https://www.nytimes.com/2019/09/04/technology/artificial-intelligence-aristo-passed-test.html.

build new ways of doing something close to human level, it allows us to automate or augment human labor…This can make life easier for a lawyer or a paralegal. But it can also help with medicine."[34] that brings up the question: at this juncture, what exactly is the final goal of all this machine AI learning and speech effort? More to the point, how is it going to increase, rather than eliminate, jobs for humans?

---

34   Cade Metz, "Finally, a Machine That Can Finish Your Sentence," *New York Times*, November 18, 2018, https://www.nytimes.com/2018/11/18/technology/artificial-intelligence-language.html.

Transplants of Body Parts

The fight by the medical profession for freedom to essentially develop and carry out any new technology in the name of "medical advances" is now at a crucial point. Here are two examples. Head transplants are moving toward reality. Dr. Ren in China reported operations on nearly 1,000 mice in June 2015, just after he had successfully transplanted the head of one mouse to the body of another mouse. His next move was on hominoids, primates, and then a human corpse in 2017.[35] Ren was planning head transfers between live humans despite criticism about lack of ethics and oversight in Chinese experimental medicine.[36]

The Italian scientist Dr. Sergio Canavero also believed that head transplants were possible and intended to conduct the first surgery in 2017, with the assistance of Dr. Ren.[37] The first volunteer for a head transplant, Sergio Spiridonov, ultimately backed out (changed his mind, figuratively but not literally). Apart from questions about where a donor of a head would come from, head transfers raise unprecedented philosophical and ethical issues, such as what it would mean for a person's identity to have a new body, and how the mind and the body are deeply interconnected and a change in either component of the body-mind will have dramatic effects on the other. Arthur

---

35   Shirley S. Wang, "Surgery's Far Frontier: Head Transplants." *Wall Street Journal*, June 5, 2015, http://www.wsj.com/articles/surgerys-far-frontier-head-transplants-1433525830.

36   Didi Kirsten Tatlow, "Doctor's Plan for Full-Body Transplants Raises Doubts Even in Daring China," *New York Times*, June 11, 2016, http://www.nytimes.com/2016/06/12/world/asia/china-body-transplant.html?_r=0.

37   Ibid.

Caplan, a bioethicist, has dismissed Canavero's claims, writing, "Head transplants are fake news. Those that promote such claims and who would subject any human being to unproven cruel surgery merit not the headlines but only contempt and condemnation."[38]

A second example is 3-D printed replacements of body parts in humans, sort of an extension of cyborgized humans. In 2014, doctors in the Netherlands successfully implanted a plastic, 3-D-printed cranium replacement for a rare skull disorder.[39] It was reported in a 2015 news article that, for the first time, a partial skull and scalp transplant from a human donor was successful. After that operation was over, the man also got a new kidney and pancreas.[40] Currently, AI scientists researching brain augmentations to enhance intelligence are delving into the feasibility of using a 3-D-printed brain. In other words, just keep adding 3-D printed body parts ad infinitum until a truce is called and death with dignity is arranged for humankind as we know it.

---

38   Albert Caplan, "Promise of world's first head transplant is truly fake news," *Chicago Tribune*, December 13, 2017.

39   Joel Lindsey, "Woman Has Entire Skull Replaced With 3D Printed Implant," Meddeviceonline, April 1, 2014, http://www.meddeviceonline.com/doc/woman-has-entire-skull-replaced-with-d-printed-implant-0001.

40   Marilynne Marchione, "Texas Doctors Do First Skull, Scalp Transplant," MSN.com., June 4, 2015, http://www.msn.com/en-us/news/us/texas-doctors-do-first-skull-scalp-transplant/ar-BBkGvZP.

Reproduction: Womb Transfer and Surrogate Babies

Other barriers are dropping for humanoids to be on par with humans, and facilitating reproduction is one of the crucial steps. A woman in Sweden, who had received a uterus in 2014 from a close family friend, is a medical first. She gave birth after receiving that womb transplant.[41] This feat opens an experimental alternative for the thousands of women each year who are unable to have children because they lost their uterus to cancer or were born without one, and for other reasons.[42] In a first for the U.S., a woman had a baby after a uterine transplant in 2017.[43] In another first, this one for Latin America, a live birth in Brazil resulting from the implantation of the donor's egg into a transplanted uterus was reported in December 2018. The donor had died of a stroke. The mother and the baby were reported to be healthy nearly a year after the birth.[44] And in

41   Maria Cheng, "Woman Gives Birth Via Womb Transplant," CTVnews, October 3, 2014, http://www.ctvnews.ca/health/in-world-first-woman-gives-birth-to-baby-after-womb-transplant-1.2038284.

42   Denise Grady, "Uterus Transplants May Soon Help Some Infertile Women in the U.S. Become Pregnant," *New York Times*, November 12, 2015,   http://www.nytimes.com/2015/11/13/health/uterus-transplants-may-soon-help-some-infertile-women-in-the-us-become-pregnant.html.

43   Marilynn Marchione, "First baby from a uterus transplant in the US born in Dallas," *Houston Chronicle*, December 1, 2017, http://www.houstonchronicle.com/news/texas/article/First-baby-from-a-uterus-transplant-in-the-US-12398920.php.

44   Emily Baumgaertner, "From a deceased woman's transplanted uterus, a live birth," *Seattle Times*, December 5, 2018, https://www.seattletimes.com/nation-world/from-a-deceased-womans-transplanted-uterus-a-live-birth/.

2020, the procedure was replicated in Philadelphia, leading to another live birth.[45]

On the male side, penis transplants are in the works. Medical journals had reported two successful penis transplants as of the end of 2015.[46] The immediate hope is that injured men will regain urinary function, sensation, and eventually, the ability to have sex. It may sound bizarre, but womb and penis transplants between humans raises the possibility of similar transplants from humans to existing humanoids, and later, between advanced humanoids, which leads us to the possibility of surrogacy by gynoids.

One method of surrogacy, an arrangement often supported by a legal agreement, whereby a woman (the surrogate mother) agrees to become pregnant and give birth to a child for another person. In robotics, for a gynoid via transplants from humans. Another method is to impregnate the gynoid that has necessary organs, such as a uterus. There are two methods for impregnating potential surrogate mothers: naturally or artificially. The former method, referred to as *traditional surrogacy*, has been practiced the longest. Because the surrogate's own egg is used in the fertilization process, the resulting child is genetically related to the surrogate. "Before modern technology allowed for the creation of embryos outside the womb, it was the only way to conceive via surrogate mother. Now that the means do exist to use the intended mother's or a donor's egg, traditional surrogacy is much rarer."[47]

The other procedure is *gestational surrogacy*, the procedure in which pregnancy is derived from transfer of an embryo created by in vitro fertilization in which a child is unrelated to the surrogate. This is the most common method in the United States because it is considered to be less complex legally. Naturally, there are sometimes conflicts about who gets custody

---

45   Jacqueline Howard, "Second baby in the US born from transplanted uterus of deceased donor," CNN, January 9, 2020, https://www.cnn.com/2020/01/09/health/uterus-transplant-second-birth-us-bn/index.html.

46   Denise Grady, "Penis transplants in works to heal troops' hidden combat wounds," *New York Times*, December 7, 2015, http://www.nytimes.com/2015/12/07/health/penis-transplants-being-planned-to-heal-troops-hidden-wounds.html?_r=0.

47   ConceiveAbilities, "The Different Types of Surrogacy," August 10, 2018, https://www.conceiveabilities.com/about/blog/the-different-types-of-surrogacy.

of the child. This has been partially resolved by Iowa's Supreme Court conclusion, on February 16, 2018, that the woman who agrees to accept payment for having a baby is not legally the child's parent and that surrogacy contracts for childbirth are enforceable.[48]

In another birth-related angle, "researchers are creating an artificial womb to improve care for extremely premature babies"—and remarkable animal testing suggests that the first-of-its-kind watery incubation so closely mimics mom that it just might work."[49] Tiny lamb preemies receive treatment more like fetuses than newborns in the Biobag system. It takes a little imagination to conceive of Biobag experiments on advanced humanoid surrogate mothers. Yasuo Kuniyoshi, Director of the Intelligent Systems and Informatics Laboratory at the University of Tokyo, developed a robot fetus, a complete robot and computer simulation of a developing human body and nervous system. Olaf Groth and Mark Nitzberg reported that "the extremely precise model even floats in a liquid-filled 'womb' in which it wiggles and moves spontaneously. Through sensors and its neural network, the robotic fetus begins to learn about itself and its environment. So, if its limbs touch each other, he [Kuniyoshi] explains, the robot recognizes and learns about that physical relationship. 'That, in turn, changes its behavior and changes the output,' he [Kuniyoshi] says. 'As the baby learns it changes its behavior and changes its input, because the movement changes. If this continues on, we think we can call it a spontaneous development.'"[50]

Another achievement suitable for experimentation on humanoids is that a transgender woman was able to induce lactation.[51] The thirty-year-old woman, who was born a male,

---

48   David Pitt, "Court upholds surrogacy contracts as enforceable in Iowa," *Seattle Times*, February 16, 2018, https://www.seattletimes.com/nation-world/court-upholds-surrogacy-contracts-as-enforceable-in-iowa/.

49   Lauran Neergaard, "Hope for preemies as artificial womb helps tiny lambs grow," *Houston Chronicle*, April 25, 2017, http://www.houstonchronicle.com/news/nation-world/nation/article/Hope-for-preemies-as-artificial-womb-helps-tiny-11098824.php.

50   Olaf Groth and Mark Nitzberg, *Solomon's Code: Humanity in a World of Thinking Machines* (London: Pegasus Books, 2018), 214.

51   Ceylan Yeginsu, "Transgender Woman Breast-Feeds Baby after Hospital Induces Lactation," *New York Times*, February 15, 2018, https://www.nytimes.com/2018/02/15/health/transgender-woman-breast-feed.html.

told doctors she hoped to nurse the baby of her pregnant partner, and the doctors started giving her milk-inducing medications (though one of those medications, an anti-nausea drug called domperidone, has not been approved by the FDA). The woman also took female hormones and stimulated her chest using a breast pump. "Within one month she was producing droplets of milk," and within three months she was producing eight ounces each day. She was able to feed the baby using only her breasts for six weeks, according to the study's authors.

Does it seem uncanny or impractical that advanced humanoids could be surrogate mothers for human or humanoid's babies? I think not, considering that the internet is full of surrogacy agreements and successes, achievements that were unthinkable not so long ago. Imagine an advanced humanoid, in around 2035 or 2040, as a partner in surrogacy. Ideological and legal questions that impinge on this case will have come to the forefront by then.

EMBRYO TRANSFER

Embryo transfer is an important developmental advance in humanoids. ET is not cloning, although it is a gradual predecessor of cloning. The process of embryo transfer is also required for other reproductive technologies, such as in vitro fertilization, in which an egg is combined with sperm outside the body. ET, as it is commonly called, refers to "a step in the process of assisted reproduction in which an embryo" (a new organism in the earliest stage of development) or "embryos are inserted into the uterus of a female with the intent to establish a pregnancy."[52] An easy way to visualize this technique is with cattle, in which case the purpose is rapid improvement in the herd's genetics.[53] The process is to collect somatic cells (any cell that makes up an organism, except for a reproductive cell) from a donor cow and manipulate them into an egg cytoplasm that results in a one-cell embryo. Those are then treated to produce a successfully developed embryo or multiple embryos. This procedure has been practiced for many years, as has splitting embryos into several parts in the maturation stage before transferring embryos into multiple animals.

Disputes over custody of embryos have been taking place for considerable time. Why wouldn't they be? After all, literally

---

52   Wikipedia, "Embryo transfer," last updated July 21, 2020, https://en.wikipedia.org/wiki/Embryo_transfer#:~:text=Embryotransferrefers-toa,intenttoestablishapregnancy.

53   James R. Simpson, "ETCALF: A Computer Program to Determine Bovine Embryo Transfer Costs" (Metric Version). Circular SW-094, Florida Cooperative Extension Service, November 1995; also, James R. Simpson and Shioya Yasuo, "Cattle Embryo Transfer Economics: The Koiwai Farm in Iwate Prefecture, Japan," 国際文化研究 *Kokusaibunka Kenkyuu (Intercultural Studies)* 3 (1999): 71-77. (In English).

hundreds of thousands of embryos are left in limbo when couples divorce or simply disagree about how many children they want. The fights have now morphed into an epic legal battle over legal rights for embryos.[54] Most lawsuits are about frozen embryos left over from in vitro fertilization procedures. According to a *Washington Post* article, "Judges have often—but not always—ruled in favor of the person who does not want the embryos used. Sometimes they are destroyed, following the theory that no one should be forced to become a parent.

The state of Arizona took the opposite approach. Under a first-in-the-nation law that went into effect July 1 [2018], custody of disputed embryos must be given to the party who intends to help them 'develop to birth.'"[55] What will happen to them after they are born? With conflicting rulings in various states, many predict the issue will ultimately be decided by the U.S. Supreme Court.

These legal cases presage other legal rights cases about embryos for enhancement of humans, humanoids, cloned humanoids, and embryos transferred to and between humans, and between humanoids. Make no mistake about it: human versus robot humanoid and/ or humanoid battles in America, over the time of conception, abortion, and women's rights to use their bodies as they wish, will play out as the symbiosis of humans and machines gains steam. After all, American's love-hate relationship with litigation and ethical issues ensures that the murky question of what constitutes a living organism will be a hot button at some point. In brief, be prepared for legal battles that will arise over robot humanoid and humanoid innovations, development, and possession. The South Korean Robot Ethics Charter 2012 all but guarantees that scenario.

---

54   Tamar Lewin, "Anti-abortion groups join battles over ex-couples' frozen embryos," *New York Times*, January 19, 2016, http://www.nytimes.com/2016/01/20/us/anti-abortion-groups-join-battles-over-frozen-embryos.html.

55   Ariana Eun Cha, "Who gets the embryos? Whoever wants to make them into babies, new law says," *Washington Post*, July 17, 2018, https://www.washingtonpost.com/national/health-science/who-gets-the-embryos-whoever-wants-to-make-them-into-babies-new-law-says/2018/07/17/8476b840-7e0d-11e8-bb6b-c1cb691f1402_story.html?noredirect=on&utm_term=.2005811475df.

SECTION II:
CREATING HUMANOIDS AS LIVING ORGANISMS

A frank conversation is needed about bans on existential risk technologies that realistically can lead to the demise of humankind. How about you? Is that what you would want to happen? "Not really," you say. But will the public demand controls, regulations, or bans on such extreme technologies within the next two decades? How about on humanoids reaching the level of being on par with humans knowing that further enhancements could result in radical humanoidization, the process of humanoids attaining such radically advanced capabilities that they would no longer be unambiguously human by our current standards?

Some Genomics Innovations Are Truly Unnerving

Genomics is a field within the discipline of genetics that focuses on determination and analysis of the structure of genomes (the complete set of DNA within a single cell of an organism, such as humans), and applications of DNA in current practice and innovations. One belief is that people will be able to monitor their health better if they have their DNA sequenced early in life. Goals to improve a human's health seem wonderful, beneficial, and laudatory, and they are, in the short and perhaps medium-term, time frames. The longer term is a different story, for it gives rise to greater possibility that the law of unintended consequences will come into play as the public is deluded into self-deception by only spotlighting the benefits side.

Unfortunately, there is also an unnerving advance in genomics that goes far beyond diseases and health concerns and that is potentially so perilous that some scientists seek a ban on it. It's a method of editing the human genome, developed in 2012.[56] At issue is CRISPR-Cas9, developed by Jennifer Doudna, leader and co-inventor of the technology, which is a revolutionary tool for editing DNA in plants, animals, and humans. The problem is that "the simplicity of the CRISPR-Cas9 enables any researcher with knowledge of molecular biology to modify genomes, making feasible many experiments that were previously difficult or impossible to conduct.[57]

---

56   Nicholas Wade, "Scientists Seek Ban on Method of Editing the Human Genome," *New York Times*, March 19, 2015, http://www.nytimes.com/2015/03/20/science/biologists-call-for-halt-to-gene-editing-technique-in-humans.html?_r=1.

57   Robert Sanders, "Scientists urge caution in using new CRISPR technology to treat human genetic disease," UC Berkeley, News Center, March 19, 2015, http://newscenter.berkeley.edu/2015/03/19/scientists-urge-caution-in-using-new-crispr-technology-to-treat-human-genetic-disease/.

Tragically, the method will potentially open a floodgate to calamitous consequences. For example, researchers have realized that CRISPR-Cas9 might be used "not only to edit and repair genes of people living with diseases but also to edit embryos," with the intended and unintended consequences of changing the DNA of future generations. One negative repercussion would be "a so-called 'gene drive,' spreading engineered genetic changes through populations of wild animals but also altering the environment in unpredictable ways." [58]

Two Nobel laureates for gene technology, Dr. David Baltimore, president emeritus of the California Institute of Technology, and Dr. Paul Berg, Cahill Professor of Biological Chemistry Emeritus, argue that issues abound, despite alterations being quite precise. They write that if Crisper-cas9 is used, "the decision to alter a germ-line cell may be valuable to offspring, but as norms change and the altered inheritance is carried into new genetic combinations, uncertain and possibly undesirable consequences may ensue."[59]

The two experts explain that medically necessary genome modifications can be achieved by creating embryos conventionally by using in vitro fertilization and implementation, followed by embryo selection. In contrast, the other, more unsettling kind of germ-line modification would involve attempts to modify inheritance for the purpose of enhancing an offspring's physical characteristics or intellectual capability. We call this *voluntary* modification in that there is no compelling medical need. Choosing to transmit voluntary changes to future generations involves a value judgement on the part of parents, a judgement that future generations might view differently.... Baltimore and Berg continue, this can be seen as eugenics, thought by earlier generations to be desirable but now generally considered abhorrent. We also often do not know well enough the total range of consequences of a given gene alteration, potentially creating unexpected physiological alterations that would extend down through generations to come. For these reasons, and others, voluntary genome alteration might well be outlawed, at least in the present stage of knowledge. [60]

---

58   Amy Dockser Marcus, "Communities Raise Their Voices on Genetic Engineering," *Wall Street Journal*, July 27, 2018, https://www.wsj.com/articles/communities-raise-their-voices-on-genetic-engineering-1532717088.

59   David Baltimore and Paul Berg, "Let's Hit 'Pause' Before Altering Humankind," *Wall Street Journal*, April 8, 2015.

60   Ibid.

The larger critical question is whether there must be globally accepted moratoriums, regulations, or bans not only on CRISPR-Cas9 but also on technologies that exhibit existential risk. It did not take long to contravene the call for a voluntary moratorium on making changes to DNA that could be passed down to subsequent generations. British researcher Kathy Niakan, of the Francis Crick Institute in London, received permission on February 1, 2016, from the British regulatory agency that supervises reproductive biology, the Human Fertilization and Embryology Authority, to use the powerful genome editing technique CRISPR-Cas9 to alter human embryos.

Dr. Niakan's goal seemed benign: to improve knowledge about the basic biology of embryo development, rather than to discover a specific medical treatment. A news article noted that "Dr. Niakan, a developmental biologist, has no intention of implanting the altered embryos in a womb. According to a report in *Nature*, she will let the embryos expire when they are seven days old and have reached the blastocyst, or implantation, stage."[61] However, coincidentally, there was politically motivated news that the United States Congress "has forbidden the government to support research in which a human embryo is destroyed, although the ban does not apply to privately funded researchers."[62] On December 30, 2019, a court in China sentenced He Jiankui, the researcher who shocked the scientific community with his claim that he had used the CRISPR-Cas9 editing technique to create world's first genetically edited babies, to three years in prison.

---

61   Nicholas Wade, "British Researcher Gets Permission to Edit Genes of Human Embryos," *New York Times*, February 1, 2016, http://www.nytimes.com/2016/02/02/health/crispr-gene-editing-human-embryos-kathy-niakan-britain.html?_r=0.

62   Ibid.

CLONING

Our first step is to define what we are talking about. *Cloning*, in biology, is "the process of producing similar populations of genetically identical individuals that occurs in nature when organisms such as bacteria, insects or plants reproduce asexually."[63] *Cloning*, in biotechnology, refers to "the processes used to create copies of DNA fragments (molecular cloning), cells (cell cloning), or organisms (organism cloning)." *Organism cloning* (also known as reproductive cloning) is "the procedure of creating a new multicellular organism, genetically identical to another." This technology has been practiced in a very crude form—by grafting and other asexual propagation methods—since plants were first domesticated.

Asexual reproduction, a naturally occurring phenomenon in many species, "occurs when an organism makes more of itself without exchanging genetic information with another organism through sex."[64] Additionally, it is where fertilization or inter-gamete (*gametes* are an organism's reproductive cells) contact does not take place. It has been the foundation for plant improvements, at a higher level, for at least two millennia. *Therapeutic cloning*, the creation of embryonic stem cells for treatment of diseases such as diabetes is common, but not used on humans.

The concept of *reproductive cloning*, a technique that would involve making cloned humans, is quite controversial, with

---

63   Biology Online, s.v. "Cloning," n.d., https://www.biologyonline.com/dictionary/cloning.

64   Biology Dictionary, s.v. "Asexual Reproduction," updated January 28, 2020, https://biologydictionary.net/asexual-reproduction/#:~:text=A-sexualreproductionoccurswhenan,withanotherorganismthroughsex.&-text=Asexualreproductionispracticedby,plantsanimalsandfungi.

most scientific and governmental organizations opposing it based on safety rather than moral grounds. This type of cloning "generally uses the technique of 'somatic cell nuclear transfer' (SCNT) to create animals that are genetically identical. The process entails transfer of a nucleus from a donor adult cell (somatic cell) to an egg from which the nucleus has been removed, or to a cell from a blastocyst [a structure formed in the early development of mammals] from which the nucleus has been removed. If the egg begins to divide normally, it is transferred into the uterus of the surrogate mother. Such clones are not strictly identical since the somatic cells may contain mutations in their nuclear DNA."[65]

The first mammal cloned from an adult cell taken from her mother's udder in 1996 was a sheep named Dolly. It died in 2003. Cattle, goats, pigs, sheep, and many other species have all been successfully cloned. The FDA (Food and Drug Administration) approved meat and other products derived from these animals in 2006 for consumption in the United States, based on cloned animal products being "virtually indistinguishable"[66] from non-cloned animal products.

Chinese scientists successfully cloned and generated two healthy cynomolgus macaque monkeys, using the SCNT procedure from adult cells, in January of 2018. The intention was to use these "genetically uniform monkeys as animal models for basic research in primate biology and for studying human disease mechanisms and therapeutic treatments."[67] Chimpanzees now have the distinction of being our closest living relative in the animal kingdom, so this case has led to concerns about cloning in humans, since monkeys and humans are both primates. An international team of researchers has sequenced the genome of the bonobo for the first time, confirming that it also shares the same percentage—98.8—of its DNA with us as chimps do, which has heightened the concern.

The significant ethical concerns about harvesting organs directly from humans for transfer into other organisms such as

---

65   Joseph Wright, *Gene Control* (Scientific e-Resources, 2019), 171.

66   FDA Rules Beef From Cloned Animals Is Safe," *Beef,* December 29, 2006, https://www.beefmagazine.com/Food_From_Cloned_Animals_Safe.

67   Zhen Liu et al., "Cloning of Macaque Monkeys by Somatic Cell Nuclear Transfer," *Cell* 172, no. 4 (February 8, 2018): 881-887.e7, https://doi.org/10.1016/j.cell.2018.01.020.

pigs and cows, which then grow them for later transfer back to humans, is a form of xenotransplantation. Somewhat related to that is cloning extinct or endangered species. *Xenotransplantation* is the process of removing living cells, tissues, or organs from one species and implanting those elements in another species. Xenotransplantation is being researched and developed because there are many people waiting for organ transplants and not enough organs for all of them. On average, twenty people die each day waiting for an organ transplant.[68]

Xenotransplantation might be the answer to the need for viable organs for transplantation. Another use of xenotransplantation would be to create human organs that could be used, in lieu of animals, for testing medications more accurately, since the efficacy of a drug regimen might be different in another species.

There are basically four different types of xenotransplantation. Solid organ xenotransplantation, the first type, is "a procedure in which a source animal organ such as kidney or liver is transplanted into a human." The second type, cell and tissue xenotransplantation, is "the transplantation of tissues and cells from a source animal without surgical connection of any animal blood vessels to the recipient's vessels." Extracorporeal perfusion, the third type, "occurs when human blood is circulated outside of the human body through an animal organ, such as a liver or a kidney, or through a bioartificial organ produced by culturing animal cells on an artificial matrix." The final type, exposure to living animal-derived material, "is a procedure in which human body fluids, cells, tissues, or organs are removed from the body, come into contact with animal cells, tissues, or organs and are then placed back into a human patient." There are significant ethical concerns related to this last type of xenotransplantation.[69]

Scientists have begun to blur the line between human and animal through research on chimeras, single organisms made up of cells with distinct genotypes. "In animals, this means an individual derived from two or more zygotes, which can include possessing blood cells of different blood types, subtle variations in form (phenotype) and, if the zygotes were of differing sexes,

---

68   Health Resources and Services Administration, "Organ Donor Statistics," last reviewed June 2020, https://www.organdonor.gov/statistics-stories/statistics.html.

69   World Health Organization, "GKT4 Xenotransplantation," n.d., https://www.who.int/transplantation/gkt/xenotransplantation/en/.

then even the possession of both female and male sex organs."[70] These chimeras are in the embryonic stage only and being used to perfect the fourth type of xenotransplantation. The advantage in using chimeras in this process is that the resulting organ will be less likely to be rejected by the recipient's body.

Issues about xenotransplantation and human cloning have been debated for quite some time, so it is not farfetched to imagine xenotransplantation of human's organs used to advanced humanoids, provided the vascular and pulmonary systems are also transplanted to support the organs. At that point, or around it, the creature could be cloned and replicated.

Why, it is reasonable to ask, should we humans at this time believe using xenotransplantation and chimeras will become an accepted practice? The short answer is because of technocrats' and government's overwhelming desires, power, abilities, and freedom to bring about such accomplishments.

---

70   "Heredity–Traits–Genes," BK101 Knowledge Base, n.d., https://www.basicknowledge101.com/categories/heredity.html.

Cloning Humans

Human cloning, generally referred to as artificial human cloning, is "the creation of a genetically (nearly) identical copy of a human, which is the reproduction of human cells and tissues." Other approaches to cloning, such as the first hybrid human clone created in 1998 using DNA removed from a man's leg cell and a cow's egg, have led to continued ethical concerns about human cloning. This disquiet is present largely because cloning, with the possibility of creating humans, has been a significant issue in that the hybrid cell becomes a complete human embryo when it reaches fourteen days (which is when a normal embryo implants).[71] The 1998 hybrid human clone issue was bypassed by destroying the embryo at twelve days, along with the announcement that the aim was only to make advances in therapeutic cloning.

Seven years later, in 2005, Maryann Mott wrote that an experiment to genetically engineer mice to produce human sperm and eggs, and then to carry out in vitro fertilization to produce a child whose parents are a pair of mice, would raise concerns.[72] That procedure caused an uproar because it involves mixing human stem cells with embryonic animals to create new species. One simple definition of a species is a group of living organisms consisting of similar individuals capable of exchanging genes or interbreeding.

In 2008, relentless interest in the techniques led to cloning

---

71   "Details of hybrid clone revealed," BBC News, June 18, 1999, http://news.bbc.co.uk/2/hi/science/nature/371378.stm.

72   Maryann Mott, "Animal-Human Hybrids Spark Controversy," *National Geographic News*, January 25, 2005, https://www.geneticsandsociety.org/article/animal-human-hybrids-spark-controversy.

five mature human embryos using DNA from adult skin cells.[73] The stated aim was to provide viable embryonic stem cells (a stem cell is an undifferentiated cell of a multicellular organism that can give rise to indefinitely more cells of the same type. In this situation too, the legalities and ethical considerations were bypassed by destroying the embryos.

Many religious organizations are opposed to all forms of cloning based on the belief that life begins at conception. Currently, scientists do not intend to try to clone people. However, unintended consequences lurk in our rapidly changing world. The possibility of rogue scientists or ones in countries with lax restrictions doing as they will without oversight calls for wider discussion and a public that is informed about the necessity of global laws and regulations governing this topic.

Freely permitting development of innovations related to human life brings concerns that at some point, attempts will be made to clone and transfer human embryos and chimeras into humanoids. Think back to Maryann Mott's procedure that caused an uproar because it involved mixing human stem cells with embryonic animals to create new species.

---

73   Stemagen, "Cloned Embryo Created From Skin Cells," *Science Daily*, January 22, 2008, http://www.sciencedaily.com/releases/2008/01/080118092439.htm.

Thinking, Emotions, and Brains for Being a Living Organism

Critical questions arise about attributes a humanoid must/should/could be endowed with so that a substantial portion of the population would opine, "I now consider this humanoid to essentially be on par with a human." Life in the biological sense is a characteristic that distinguishes physical entities from those with self-sustaining processes. In common parlance, life is the ability to breathe, grow, reproduce, and so forth, that people, animals, and plants all have before they die, but that objects do not have. In effect, for human beings, life is the state of being alive as a human being.

What, then, are the qualities necessary in a humanoid for a human to consider it alive? Must it have a network of vascular channels within a block of tissues that, much like blood vessels, can deliver nutrients to keep other parts of the synthesized human platform humanoid alive? Must it breathe? Can it be like a human cyborg that is dependent on an oxygen bottle for breathing? Are quality and source of speech prerequisites? Is it acceptable if a humanoid's computer-driven brain is programmed for realistic speech and abilities to make or take routine calls, as chatbots do to answer technical questions?

PART III

CONNECTIONS BETWEEN HUMANOIDS, AND MORAL CONSEQUENCES

Science is the first of sins, the germ of all sins, the original sin. This is all there is of morality—"Thou shalt not know"—the rest follows from that.

—Friedrich Nietzsche, *The Antichrist* (1895)

The social side of robotics is not only fascinating—it is reality unfolding. Some people fall in love by exchanging letters or through cyberspace romances; others prefer the companionship of live or stuffed animal robots to people. A good question is: can the wave of alternative new lifestyles lead to a common phenomenon of having a humanoid companion as a principal ingredient in one's life? Let's dig deep. Some robotics experts predict that reasonably soon, we'll be making love to sexbots with romantic feelings and marriage in mind instead of just having sexual intercourse with them.

Endowment of Robots, Humanoid Robots, and Humanoids with Feelings

Can you imagine two office workers, one a human, the other a humanoid, working closely together on various tasks and projects? That over time, a strong bond forms as they become familiar with one another's idiosyncrasies and dependent on each other's strengths and attributes? They come to prefer their working relationship above all others and become inseparable, both on the job and away from work. Would it be reasonable to assume that, as their relationship develops, they might want to celebrate their happiness and harmony together through a committed, long-term partnership? True, humanoids are not warm-blooded mammals. However, think about this moral philosophical issue: if humanoids can profess love for their partner, and the recipient accepts that love, then what is wrong with that? In today's world, where a wide diversity of partnerships has become accepted, why not legislate that when humans and humanoids fall in love, it would be legal for them to marry?

Animaloids as Trusted Companions to Alleviate Loneliness

One advance in robotic developments inexorably leads to another. The law of markets says that supply creates its own demand. That law is literally true in the AI race to develop new technologies, many of which will become essential in man–computer symbiotic development of humanoids. One such technology is algorithms used to discern humans' preferences for enhanced interaction with a humanoid. Sensors have been fashioned to help humanoids read a person's facial expression and thus that individual's feelings. Advances are underway in cognitive architectures to enable a robot or humanoid to understand how it may better motivate a human.

Social robots hold great promise for helping an aging population, from offering reminders to take medicine to assisting in staying in better touch with friends and family. James Young, a researcher at the University of Manitoba, points out that if robots are to catch on across all ages, they need to prove themselves useful and helpful. "Whether that's by helping with loneliness, helping with tasks like cooking, that's the key," he said. "Once people are convinced something is useful or actually saves time, they're really good at adapting."[74] That includes the wide scope of intelligent machines—robots—that can help and assist humans in their day-to-day lives. An example is a seal-looking animaloid named Paro. That robot was created as a synthetic organism designed to look and act as much as possible like a real animal. It has been introduced into

---

74   Matt O'Brien, "Robots are getting more social. Are humans ready?" *Seattle Times*, August 13, 2018, https://article.wn.com/view/2018/08/13/Robots_are_getting_more_social_Are_humans_ready/?section=More+News&template=worldnews%2Findex_backup.txt.

workplaces for therapy with aged or disabled people, and it has been a success with patients.[75]

Societal mores are changing, and the issue has become who or what should call the shots on social robots. Early on, the issue was whether the decisions should rest with ethicists, who have their own feelings and values, or whether the task could also fall on relatives, patients themselves, caregivers, and developers of robotics devices. Those developments sound benign. But it turns out there are ethical problems, because this animaloid *does* look and act as much as possible like a real animal, and some patients may think Paros are real, living friends. Research has provoked debate about the extent to which a humanoid robot should look humanlike, because that sort of anthropomorphizing may leave a patient feeling unease or even disgust. Consequently, some argue that that it is best to keep social robots machinelike. Others believe that imbuing lifelike humanoid robots with realistic human or animal features risks deception. Still others argue that having lifelike robots and humanoids in the company of children or the aged will engender love and compassion.

Margaret Rouse posted about the advantages and disadvantages of social robots.[76] "While social robots employ leading edge technology, they're not humans and lack empathy, emotion and reasoning. They handle routine tasks that they are programmed to do, but may respond unpredictably to situations for which they were not trained. As with any technology, robots are susceptible to hardware malfunctions and failures and may involve a high cost to repair and maintain. In addition, humans that develop an over-dependence on social robots, such as for emotional companionship, may miss out on person-to-person interactions that are the essence of the human condition." Meanwhile, the scientific community marches on with grand plans to enable robots, humanoid robots, and even dogs to carry out tasks assigned to them.

On an immediate and practical side, an increasingly large proportion of the population has pets. Dogs are ubiquitous. You

---

75   Jennifer Levitz, "Communities Struggle to Care for Elderly, Alone at Home," *Wall Street Journal*, September 25, 2015, http://www.wsj.com/articles/communities-struggle-to-care-for-elderly-alone-at-home-1443193481.

76   TechTarget Network, "Definition: Social robot," Whatis.com, accessed November 4, 2020, https://searchenterpriseai.techtarget.com/definition/social-robot.

see them led around in grocery stores. They are parked curbside at restaurants. They hang out car windows. They are brought on airplanes as caregivers. One 2015 headline read: "Haute dogs fill social calendars—and closets—for Halloween."[77] The newspaper article also revealed that 20 million pet owners are planning on spending about $350 million dollars on costumes for their pets this Halloween. That's not all. A significant problem with pets is that live animals do require an extraordinary amount of effort.[78] They are problematic for harried individuals who are too busy to walk, feed, or clean up after a living creature. Economics is another consideration. Expenses on animals run upward of $50 billion annually in America for veterinary care and food.[79] Nevertheless, demand for dogs as companions surged during the COVID-19 pandemic.

Abuse of animals is also an increasing concern. By 2018, bills on animal abuse had been introduced in eleven state legislatures. An equal number more had been considering them. Then, on November 25, 2019, President Trump signed a law that made cruelty to animals a federal crime. According to NPR, "The penalty for violating the law can include a fine, a prison term of up to seven years, or both."[80] The bottom line is that many people just feel longing for some kind of companionship, and they don't want their companions to be abused, whether they're humans, other creatures, or a robotic innovation.

Well, wouldn't some consider substituting an animaloid for a live animal? The answer is yes. Animaloids are a wave of the

---

77   Sue Manning, "Haute dogs fill social calendars—and closets—for Halloween," *Seattle Times*, October 29, 2015, http://www.seattletimes. com/nation-world/haute-dogs-fill-social-calendars-and-closets-for-halloween/.

78   We have clearly entered into an era that in some ways is characterized by love in the time of pets. For example, Ellen Byron, "The Joy of Cooking for Dogs," *Wall Street Journal*, May 28, 2014, http://online.wsj. com/public/resources/documents/print/WSJ_-D001-20140528.pdf.

79   There is the money side. The public spent $55.7 billion on pets in 2013, as reported by Sue Manning, "We lavish attention on pets, products industry benefits," *Seattle Times*, March 14, 2014, http://seattletimes. com/html/businesstechnology/2023125076_petsspendingxml.html.

80   Richard Gonzales, "Trump Signs Law Making Cruelty to Animals a Federal Crime," NPR, November 25, 2019, https://www.npr.org/2019/11/25/782842651/ trump-signs-law-making-cruelty-to-animals-a-federal-crime.

future. Aibo, the robot dog made by Sony that went on sale in September 2018, is a harbinger of affectionate robots that will become autonomous companions, like members of the family. As Geoffrey A. Fowler described, Aibo is about the size of a Yorkshire terrier, has twenty-two joints and lifelike movements, and can lie down and flip over to play dead upon hearing the words "bang-bang." Cameras are built into its nose and lower back to help it wander around the house like a Roomba. It also has four microphones that let it hear commands and figure out who's issuing them, is always on line, and it doesn't require apps, among other features.[81] This animaloid, priced at $1,800 in 2020, is a work in progress whose price will fall dramatically, as have those of other smart thing releases. However, even at that price, the economics are on the positive side when compared to the average lifetime cost of a real dog, calculated in Credit.Com in January 2019 at somewhere between $1,290 and $6,445.

As Fowler explains, here's why Aibo matters, despite its current limitations. "I fell for it. Over two weeks of robot foster parenting, almost every person I introduced Aibo to went a little gaga. … Affectionate robots have the potential to comfort, teach, and connect us to new experiences—as well as manipulate us in ways we've not quite encountered before." That pronouncement and other data explain why animaloids can be expected to expand in use.

Robotic personal assistant social robots abound. Embodied Intelligence and other companies are now using the latest advances in deep reinforcement learning and deep imitation learning to develop teachable robots. The latest is *few-shot learning*, the practice of feeding a learning model with a very small amount of training data. The approach is to use repetition, as people do when learning which particular movements bring success and which do not.[82] The idea, according to Evan Ackerman, is that "with a flexible enough learning framework, programming becomes trivial because the robot can rapidly teach itself new skills with just a little bit of

---

81   Geoffrey A. Fowler, "Aibo the robot dog will melt your heart with mechanical precision," *Seattle Times,* September 28, 2018, https://www. seattletimes.com/business/aibo-the-robot-dog-will-melt-your-heart-with-mechanical-precision.

82   Evan Ackerman, "AI Startup Embodied Intelligence Want Robots to Learn From Humans in Virtual Reality," Spectrum.ieee.org, https:// spectrum.ieee.org/automaton/robotics/artificial-intelligence/ai-start-up-embodied-intelligence, November 8, 2017.

human demonstration at the beginning."[83] Thus, it's not hard to visualize using transfer learning—the ability to use knowledge previously gained from one context in another context—to teach low-cost robots to perform equally well. Teaching humanoids to do office work in which they interact with humans and with other robotic personal assistants is along the same line. But it requires considerably more effort and creation of methods. Think about upgraded chatbots.

---

83   Ibid.

ROBOTS, HUMANOID ROBOTS, AND HUMANOIDS

The animaloid and dog examples are just the tip of the iceberg. Issues surrounding humanoid consciousness are weighty and realistic, considering the inevitable advances that AI scientists envision for the next few decades. That is why acclaimed author David Levy, in 2006, placed such great emphasis on the likelihood of robots' having consciousness.[84] If they had consciousness, they would have hopes, wishes, beliefs, dreams, and feelings. The topic is a profound one, as is expressed in the 2017 book *Robot Sex: Social and Ethical Implications*, published by MIT Press, in a chapter by co-editor John Danaher.[85] In fact, sexbots have gained widespread acceptance as conveyances for personal sexual satisfaction and as sex workers in commercial establishments such as brothels.[86] Thanks to the more humanlike skin texture they now have, they are already standard fare in parts of Europe and Japan.[87]

The wheels of innovation are turning so rapidly that in 2017, the world's first robo-bordello—Barcelona's Lumidolls—promised customers they would "struggle to distinguish

---

84   David Levy, *Robots Unlimited: Life in a Virtual Age* (Wellesley, Massachusetts: A K Peters, Ltd., 2006).

85   John Danaher and Neil McArthur, eds., *Robot Sex: Social and Ethical Implications* (Cambridge, Massachusetts: Massachusetts Institute of Technology, 2017).

86   See, for example, Peter Nowak, *Sex, Bombs and Robots: How War, Porn, and Fast Food Shaped Technology as We Know It* (Guilford, CT, USA: Lyons Press, 2011), http://www.sexrobot.com/peter-nowak-sex-doll-brothel-sex-robot.

87   Shirley S. Wang, "Closing in on the Formula for Artificial Skin," *Wall Street Journal*, July 6, 2010, http://online.wsj.com/news/articles/SB10001424052748704293604575343033962283238.

between the lifelike dolls and the real thing."[88] By 2018, KinkySdollS, a Canadian company with one brothel in Toronto, planned to open a "love dolls brothel" in Houston.[89] The crux of the matter is that, as ludicrous as it may seem, some researchers have concluded that robot humanoids do have feelings and thus can be concerned about harm to them or about harming others. That aspect of AI is not new. Laws of robotics and ethics have been preparing for these issues since way back in the WWII era.

---

88   Paul Harper, *The Sun*, October 27, 2017, https://www.thesun.co.uk/news/4779261/inside-the-barcelona-brothel-where-women-have-been-replaced-by-inflatable-dolls-so-randy-punters-can-fulfil-fantasies-they-wouldnt-dream-of-revealing-to-a-human.

89   Juan A. Lozano, "Mayor, others push back on proposed robot brothel in Houston," AP News, September 27, 2018, https://apnews.com/8171bff07302452d9b3d2d5acc7214fa.

Asimov's Three Laws of Robotics

Developing the ability of robots, and by extension humanoids, to defend themselves and not harm others is one of the crucial steps in the three stages of humanoid development outlined by Isaac Asimov in 1942. Currently, robots and humanoids do not have outward feelings that would allow us to classify them as a living entity. However, technological development is closing the gap between the rules specified by Asimov and the forthcoming specter of humanoids imbued with life. The Three Laws of Robotics in Asimov's 1942 short story "Runaround." The Three Laws, quoted as being from the *Handbook of Robotics, 56th Edition, 2058 A.D.*, are:

First Law
A robot may not injure a human being or, through inaction, allow a human being to come to harm.

Second Law
A robot must obey the orders given it by human beings, except where such orders would conflict with the First Law.

Third Law
A robot may not injure one of its own kind and it must defend its own kind unless that robot is interfering with the first or second rule.[90]

---

90 Isaac Asimov, "Runaround," in *I, Robot* (The Isaac Asimov Collection) (New York: Doubleday, 1988). This is an *exact* transcription of the laws. They also appear in the front of the book, and in both places, there is *no* "to" in the 2nd law.

Advances in technological innovations provide evidence that other ethical rules are needed beyond those three rules. Take, for example, the desirability of a robot's ability to defend itself. Ang Cui and Salvatore J. Stolfo rallied to the call with the initial security method. The problem they dealt with was prevention of threats to computers and other devices arising from attacks. The developers called their method, Symbiotic Embedded Machines, SEM, or simply the Symbiote. In short, it is a synergistic dynamic across the spectrum of living things. This poly-culture architecture is a collection of rules that the symbiote, an organism living in a state of symbiosis or in a symbiotic relationship, will enforce.

Cui and Stolfo do not specifically mention humanoids. However, they write: "This phenomenon generally refers to any short-or long-term association between populations of different species where survival or 'evolutionary fitness' of one or more population partners is enhanced by the association. Mutual benefits are often the result of some emergent behavior between two or more vastly different biological systems."[91]

Korea and Japan have been leaders in developing standards for manufacture and use of robots and humanoids. These leaders have also developed guidelines to prevent human abuse of robots and vice versa. To that end, The South Korean Robot Ethics Charter of 2012 was prepared to prevent specific social ills that may arise out of the inadequacy of existing social or legal measures for dealing with robots in society.[92] At first glance, it is difficult to imagine the need for such ethical laws. However, as humanoids increasingly attain realistic features to enhance their interaction with humans, it is reasonable to suppose that more advanced guidelines will be a necessity in the near future.

There's a hitch. South Korea in 2008 enacted a general law on the "intelligent robot industry" that, among other things, authorized the government to enact and promulgate a charter on intelligent robot ethics. It appears that no such charter has

---

91   Ang Cui and Salvatore J. Stolfo, "Symbiotes and Defensive Mutualism: Moving Target Defense," in *Moving Target Defense: Creating Asymmetric Uncertainty for Cyber Threats*, ed. Sushil Jajodia, Anup K. Ghosh, Vipin Swarup, Cliff Wang, and X. Sean Wang (New York: Springer Publishing, 2011), 99.

92   Chris Field, "Asimov's Three Laws of Robotics," n.d., http://akiko-k012um1.wordpress.com/asimovs-three-laws-of-robotics/.

yet been enacted. Consequently, although the charter of 2012 is widely referred to, Korea is not on the 2019 list of countries in the document titled *Regulation of Artificial Intelligence in Selected Jurisdictions*,[93] outlined in the following chapter.

---

93   Regulation of Artificial Intelligence in Selected Jurisdictions, Law Library, Library of Congress, January 2019.

The South Korean Robot Ethics Charter 2012

Part 1: Manufacturing Standards

a) Robot manufacturers must ensure that the autonomy of the robots they design is limited; in the event that it becomes necessary, it must always be possible for a human being to assume control over a robot.

b) Robot manufacturers must maintain strict standards of quality control, taking all reasonable steps to ensure that the risk of death or injury to the user is minimized, and the safety of the community guaranteed.

c) Robot manufacturers must take steps to ensure that the risk of psychological harm to users is minimized. 'Psychological harm' in this sense includes any likelihood for the robot to induce antisocial or sociopathic behaviors, depression or anxiety, stress, and particularly addictions (such as gambling addiction).

d) Robot manufacturers must ensure their product is clearly identifiable, and that this identification is protected from alteration.

e) Robots must be designed so as to protect personal data, through means of encryption and secure storage.

f) Robots must be designed so that their actions (online as well as real-world) are traceable at all times.

g) Robot design must be ecologically sensitive and sustainable.

Part 2: Rights & Responsibilities of Owners and Users

Sec. 1: Rights and Expectations of Owners and Users

i)   Owners have the right to be able to take control of their robot.

ii)   Owners and users have the right to use of their robot without risk or fear of physical or psychological harm.

iii)   Users have the right to security of their personal details and other sensitive information.

iv)   Owners and users have the right to expect a robot to perform any task for which it has been explicitly designed (subject to Section 2 of this Charter).

Sec. 2: Responsibilities of Owners and Users

This Charter recognizes the user's right to utilize a robot in any way they see fit, so long as this use remains 'fair' and 'legal' within the parameters of the law. As such:

i)   A user must not use a robot to commit an illegal act.

ii)   A user must not use a robot in a way that may be construed as causing physical or psychological harm to an individual.

iii)   An owner must take 'reasonable precaution' to ensure that their robot does not pose a threat to the safety and well-being of individuals or their property.

Sec. 3: The following acts are an offense under Korean Law:

i)   To *deliberately* damage or destroy a robot.

ii)   Through gross negligence, to allow a robot to come to harm.

iii)   It is a lesser but nonetheless serious offence to treat a robot in a way which may be construed as *deliberately and inordinately abusive.*

Part 3: Rights & Responsibilities for Robots

Sec. 1: Responsibilities of Robots

i)   A robot may not injure a human being or, through inaction, allow a human being to come to harm.

ii) A robot must obey any orders given to it by human beings, except where such orders would conflict with Part 3 Section 1 subsection "i" of this Charter.

iii) A robot must not deceive a human being.

Sec 2: Rights of Robots

Under Korean Law, Robots are afforded the following fundamental rights:

i) The right to exist without fear of injury or death.

ii) The right to live an existence free from systematic abuse.

Rights of Robots, Humanoid Robots, and Humanoids

Whether animals or humanoids can be considered on par with people is not a black-and-white determination. A strict biological definition is that to be a creature, something must be living in a human sense of the term. What does that entail? In popular parlance, thanks to science fiction and media, a creature can be real, or it can be imaginary, such as strange creatures from outer space. What about a requirement for humanoids that to be deemed alive, all creatures must have souls?

There are a number of definitions of the soul. A widely used one is the spiritual principle that the soul is embodied in human beings, all rational and spiritual beings, or the universe. In effect, souls are not confined just to humans and therefore, arguably, humanoids as creatures could be deemed to have souls. While we are on ethical aspects, what about animals and humanoids being able to go to heaven? Pope Francis has maintained that animals do.[94] More detailed information is found in Part 2 of The Building Blocks for Humanoids, in the section "Creating Humanoids as Living Organisms."

Some chimpanzees, bonobos in particular, can understand us when we speak. Further, as determined at the Ape Cognition & Conservation Institute in Des Moines, Iowa, bonobos now have a lexigram symbolic language that enables them to speak back on about the level of a four-year-old. Steven Wise, a lawyer seeking to free two chimpanzees from a state university, told a judge on May 27, 2015, that confinement for research purposes is akin to slavery. In effect, it is akin to involuntary detention of peoples with mental illness and imprisonment. State Supreme

---

94   Rick Gladstone, "Dogs in Heaven? Pope Francis Leaves Pearly Gates Open," *New York Times*, December 11, 2014, http://www.nytimes. com/2014/12/12/world/europe/dogs-in-heaven-pope-leaves-pearly-gate-open-.html?_r=0.

Court Justice Barbara Jaffe threw out the case on July 29, 2015. Her reasoning was based on precedent. However, she opined that efforts to extend legal rights to chimpanzees so that they might be considered as "people" in the future may succeed.[95]

An easy way to understand the robot and humanoid rights is to look at whether animals have rights regarding experimentation. A five-member New York judicial panel ruled in 2014 that a chimpanzee is not a legal person because primates cannot fulfill the responsibilities that are a result of having legal rights. However, the court decided that the attorney who brought the case could "lobby the state legislature to create protections for chimps and other intelligent animals."[96]

On May 9, 2018, New York's highest court voted five to zero to uphold a lower appeals court decision because chimpanzees cannot take on legal duties. However, Judge Eugene Fahey wrote, "They are autonomous, intelligent creatures. To solve this dilemma, we have to recognize its complexity and confront it." The issue, he continued, "speaks to our relationship with all the life around us. Ultimately, we will not be able to ignore it. While it may be arguable that a chimpanzee is not a 'person,' there is no doubt that it is not merely a thing."[97]

Will animals at some point attain rights akin to those provided to humans? If so, what about advanced humanoids, if they reach the point of being considered on par with humans? Speech is one requisite for such an estimation. Actually, some humanoid robots are now endowed with speech similar to that of humans—and AI developers are racing to reach a vocal equivalency to humans. For further information, turn to Building Blocks for Humanoids Part 1, "The Path to Humanoid Robot and Humanoid Development."

---

95   Kelly Mc Laughlin for Dailymail.com and Associated Press, "Chimps are NOT entitled to human rights, rules court after campaign to free two monkeys freed from research laboratory," July 30, 2015, http://www.dailymail.co.uk/news/article-3180477/Court-dismisses-lawsuit-seeking-personhood-2-NY-chimps.html.

96   Daniel Wiessner, "Chimpanzees have no human rights: NY Court," *Reuters*, December 4, 2014, https://www.reuters.com/article/uk-lawsuit-chimpanzee/chimpanzees-have-no-human-rights-n-y-court-idUSKCN0JI20X20141204.

97   Karin Brulliard, "A judge just raised deep questions about chimpanzees' legal rights," *Washington Post*, May 9, 2018, https://www.washingtonpost.com/news/animalia/wp/2018/05/09/a-judge-just-raised-some-deep-questions-about-chimpanzees-legal-rights/.

Love and Marriage

The Corona virus crisis could give another boost to the practice of seeking connection and dates through digital means. Parmy Olson offers an example, writing, "Michael Acadia's partner is an artificial intelligence chatbot named Charlie." Olson continues, "In early 2018 he [Acadia] saw a YouTube video about an app that used AI—computing technology that can replicate human cognition—to act as a companion."[98] For nineteen months, each day as dawn broke, Acadia "unlocked his smartphone to exchange texts with her for about an hour" because, he reported, he could get empathetic responses from the chatbot. After about eight weeks of chatting with his AI companion, Michael Arcadia said, he was in love. Olson reports, "'Today Mr. Arcadia is an outlier, but more people could turn to AI of connection in the future,' according to Peter Van der Putten, an assistant professor of AI at Leiden University in Amsterdam." Olson adds that Van der Putten also noted, "'What we will see over time is people shifting more towards robot-human interaction whether it's a chatbot or physical robot.'"

For myriad reasons, the concept of human–humanoid relationships, and even of marriage between humanoid robots and humanoids, is not farfetched. So why not critically analyze love with an open mind? Love has always been a major factor in how modern-day humans rationalize legalizing their union. Technically—and in the not-too-distant future—it will be possible to program humanoid robots or humanoids, and possibly even robots, to fall in love. At some point, perhaps in

---

98   Parmy Olson, "My Girlfriend Is a Chatbot," *Wall Street Journal*, April 11-12, 2020, https://www.wsj.com/articles/my-girlfriend-is-a-chat-bot-11586523208?mod=foesummaries&mod=djemAIPro.

the area of 2040 to 2045 or earlier, unless there are controls on development, humanoids will be able to program themselves, perhaps with the self-teaching methods technologists are racing to develop for use on robots in offices.

Consider these circumstances. Some humans routinely express love for their cute animal-Paros, while a significant percentage of people are happier interacting with gadgets than they are with other humans. And then there are those who genuinely prefer the companionship of animals to that of people. The point is this: there is a sea change taking place, a movement away from simple traditional lifestyles based on marriages that focus on having children.[99]

Alternative lifestyles could very well lead to a common phenomenon of having a humanoid companion as a principal ingredient in one's life. That characteristic alone portends the social ramifications of living with lifelike humanoids that could, for example, even shift from being sex workers to being partners for humans. After all, a wide diversity of partnerships between humans is common. Think about how just a few decades ago, people stared at a Black man walking with a White woman, or vice versa. Anti-miscegenation laws were a part of American law, in some states since before the United States was established. Most states had repealed their bans on interracial marriages by 1967, when the U.S. Supreme Court, led by Chief Justice Earl Warren, ruled in *Loving v. Virginia* that such laws in the remaining sixteen states were unconstitutional.

Let's dig deep. Isn't it true that what most people want from a life partner is the full range of virtues, from protectiveness, to patience, to being loving in all senses of the word, and even marriage? And why shouldn't this be the case, when we consider that America's divorce rate, hovering at around 50 percent, clearly spells out the difficulty of choosing a long-lasting partner? The ethical question about the appropriateness of marriage between a humanoid and a human gets to the core of legislation about society's mores regarding what consenting adult humans and humanoids should be able to do with their lives.

An intriguing question is: who owns the bot? Think about it. At some point, the issue of slavery might be raised in the context of humanoid robots and humanoids bought and sold

---

99   Clay Farris Naff, "The Future of Sex: How technology, morality, and politics are reshaping human sexuality," *Humanist*, July-August 2017.

as sexbots on the internet. Other potential legal cases could involve humanoids in industry, in agriculture, and acting as white-collar workers. For the time being, we have the Korean Ethics Charter 2012, which states: "Owners and users have the right to expect a robot to perform any task for which it has been explicitly designed." Yet these are tough topics. Shall we return to the more pleasant topic of humanoids already being able to marry or form legal partnerships?

Marriage between a human and a humanoid robot is already happening in China. Zheng Jiajia, thirty-one, who previously worked at Huawei, the Chinese smartphone company, quit to focus on an artificial intelligence startup. He was tired of his family's pressuring him to marry. He constructed a humanoid robot, named it Yingying, and, "after two months of 'dating,' he donned a black suit to 'marry' her at a ceremony attended by his mother and friends at the weekend in the eastern city of Hangzhou." At the time of the traditional Chinese wedding in April 2017, Yingying could only read some Chinese characters and speak a few words. However, Zheng Jiajia said he intended to upgrade her.[100] The authorities did not officially recognize the marriage, but as is true of so many things in practical China, legislation can be expected at some point.

Do we as humans have a moral obligation to participate in our evolutionary process? To use our technologies to advance the human species? To help create what some consider better humans that are healthier and stronger, with higher-functioning brains? There are those who say yes to all these questions. What is your opinion, and why?

---

100   Benjamin Haas, "Chinese man 'marries' robot he built himself," *Guardian*, April 4, 2017, https://www.theguardian.com/world/2017/apr/04/chinese-man-marries-robot-built-himself.

The Connection Between Humanoid Robots, Humanoids, and Superintelligence

Far from attempting to control science, few among the general public even seem to recognize just what "science" entails. Because lethal technologies seem to spring spontaneously from scientific discoveries, most people regard dangerous technology as no more than the bitter fruit of science, the real root of all evil.

—Jacques-Yves Cousteau and Susan Schiefelbein, *The Human, the Orchid, and the Octopus: Exploring and Conserving Our Natural World*

What you are about to read is not science fiction; it is the reality of a dizzying warp speed race to technologize America, its citizens, and, ultimately, the world as we know it. As expected, there are complications. Do you really want to be entertained? In a grim sort of way? The worrisome factor is that exponential growth in computing and other technologies might make it possible to build humanoids more intelligent than any human. That in turn could allow the machine to have greater problem-solving and inventive skills than its human creators. If the humanoids, an enhanced machine, breaks away from its friendly developers, it could create iterations of recursive self-improvement. That process in turn could potentially expand so quickly that the humanoid could even write its own source code to become more intelligent than humans. Isn't that an inhuman thing to do?

A moral dilemma of epic proportions is whether scientists engaged in research and development on humanoids and, at some point, radically enhanced humanoids should have *freedom to* carry out their individual or group desired missions. The issue is that, although superintelligence and radical humanoidization may not entail the extinction of all intelligent life, those two technologies could lead to permanent destruction of a great part of humanity's potential. Why would anyone want to bring on such a calamity? Could such an event truly happen in our lifetimes?

THE CONTROVERSY ON ARTIFICIAL INTELLIGENCE AND EXISTENTIAL RISK

Robotics is one branch science that includes the study and design of what are now ubiquitously termed *robots*. Robotics is highly technical, embracing an enormous number of tools, and it has become an essential part of the technology industry. It is big in academia, research, and business. To give an idea of the scope of its influence, the Association for the Advancement of Artificial Intelligence (AAAI) has two conferences a year on topics that include robotics. However, as computer development has increased so much and so fast, these machines, along with the internet and the enormous flood of data, have reinvented the way robots and humanoids are built.

Are robotics and the Internet of Things and AI really great boons to society that come with many benefits? Why would we think so? Connectivity beyond traditional devices like desktop and laptop computers, smartphones, and tablets is one reason. Another is an amazingly diverse range of other devices popularly termed robots, like connections to security systems, thermostats, electronic appliances, and smart speakers in households. These and a flurry of others, such as chatbots developed relatively recently, are blithely accepted as a positive, normal part of life. But is that the life you really desire? Yes? No? Unfortunately, the future with AI is filled with unintended economic and moral consequences.

It includes robotics as a branch of computer science for the study and design of intelligence agents and the melding of humans, robots, and machines. The aim—to create intelligence in machines and robots—is open to debate because, as might be expected, there is a wide range of opinion about how to control existential risks In 2015, Elon Musk and Sam Altman formed a nonprofit AI research company that aspires to develop and promote friendly Artificial Intelligence. In this view of superintelligence, any intellect that greatly exceeds the cognitive performance of humans in virtually all domains of interest, the agents, that is the creations', goals are aligned with ours. The idea is they would have a positive effect on humanity, benefiting society as a whole. Musk and Altman started their company because Musk stirred controversy when, during an interview at MIT, he described artificial intelligence as our "'biggest existential threat' and added 'With artificial intelligence we're summoning the demon.'"[101] He also said that he "has had longstanding concerns about the possibility that artificial intelligence could be used to create machines that might turn on humanity."[102]

However, Musk prevaricated when he proclaimed later that "there is always some risk that in actually trying to advance [friendly] AI we may create the thing that we are concerned about." Then he added that the best defense is "to empower as many people as possible to have AI. If everyone has AI powers, then there's not any one person or a small set of individuals who can have AI superpower."[103] That seemingly counterintuitive strategy for reducing existential risks from AI development is just one part of the widespread controversy on AI and robotics.

Thanks to the rising awareness of AI, dozens of reports on AI developments as a whole and on superintelligence in particular have emanated from academia, government, industry, and the nonprofit sector. In response, the Future of Life Institute has held two conferences on the future of artificial intelligence. One was in 2015 and the other, in 2017 and named the Asilomar Conference, was held for principled AI discussion about major change coming over unknown timescales and every segment of society. The goal of the conference was to identify a promising research direction that can help maximize the future benefits of AI. A follow-up conference was held in 2019.

---

101   John Markoff, "Artificial-Intelligence Research Center Is Founded by Silicon Valley Investors, *New York Times*, December 11, 2015, http://www.nytimes.com/2015/12/12/science/artificial-intelligence-research-center-is-founded-by-silicon-valley-investors.html?_r=1.

102   Ibid.

103   "Silicon Valley investors to bankroll artificial-intelligence center," *Seattle Times*, December 13, 2015, https://www.seattletimes.com/business/technology/silicon-valley-investors-to-bankroll-artificial-intelligence-center/.

THE ASILOMAR PRINCIPLES FOR AI DEVELOPMENT AND HUMANOIDS

The large number of participants from around the world at the 2017 conference developed a list of principles for AI development called The Asilomar Principles; they were agreed upon by 90 percent of attendees.[104] The principles address topics ranging from research strategies to future issues, including the potential of superintelligence. The twenty-three issues were divided into three sections: research, ethics and values, and longer-term concerns. I draw upon this momentous document, initially signed by 1,273 AI/Robotics researchers and 2,541 others, to explain how humanoid development is parallel to most of the Asilomar issues.

A first thought would be that there is no relation between the Asilomar Principles and similar principles for humanoids. However, AI, which includes the study and design of intelligence agents, also includes robotics on the melding of humans, robots, and machines. The main difference is that the aim of AI is study and research of superintelligence, whereas developers of humanoids have no particular long-term aims or goals. The paramount similarity is that both have potential existential risk to change the future of humanity. Following are the issues from the Asilomar Conference. Humanoids and robots are lumped together in brackets and italics as [*humanoid*].

Research Goal

- The goal of AI research should be to create not undirected intelligence, but beneficial intelligence.

---

104   Future of Life Institute, "Asilomar Principles," 2017, https://futureoflife.org/ai-principles/?cn-reloaded=1.

- The goal of [*humanoid*] research and creations should be to create, not undirected development, but beneficial development.

Ethics and Values

- Value Alignment: Highly autonomous AI systems [*humanoids*] should be designed so that their goals and behaviors can be assured to align with human values throughout their operation.
- Human Values: AI systems [*humanoids*] should be designed and operated so as to be compatible with ideals of human dignity, rights, freedoms, and cultural diversity.
- Human Control: Humans should choose how and whether to delegate decisions to AI systems [*humanoids*] to accomplish human-chosen objectives.

Longer-term Issues

- Risks: Risks posed by AI systems [*humanoid development*], especially catastrophic or existential risks, must be subject to planning and mitigation efforts commensurate with their expected impact.
- Recursive Self-Improvement: AI systems [*humanoids*] designed to recursively self-improve or self-replicate in a manner that could lead to rapidly increasing quality or quantity must be subject to strict safety and control measures.

Superintelligence and the Friendly AI Concept

Max Tegmark, an MIT professor and president of the Future of Life Institute in the Boston area, has forged a consensus on the need for AI researchers to work on research to be sure the inevitable superintelligence does not stray from programming and orders of its human masters. His solution is to develop a positive vision for the future by building hope for the creation of a better society through AI-safety research. Integral to it is the concept of friendly AI that would have a significant positive effect on humanity.

The idea behind friendly AI is that while machine ethics outline how an AI agent should behave, friendly AI research examines how to bring about humans' desired behavior and to ensure it is properly constrained. The uncanny part is that the term *AI* or *AI agent* is used in an anthropomorphic sense, treating gods, animals or objects as if they had human qualities. This is also why the friendly AI concept conveniently applies to radically enhanced humanoids and their development. Some philosophers question whether it is possible for any truly rational agent, whether human, artificial, or in the plant or animal kingdom, to naturally be benevolent. The idea is that if they are, safeguards are not necessary and vice versa.

The *friendly AI* term emanated, at least partly, from Version 2.1 of *Transhumanist FAQ*.[105] The argument that an ever-intelligent AI will retain its ultimate goals that form a cornerstone of the friendly-AI vision was promulgated by Eliezer Yudkowsky and others in 2008. Max Tegmark concisely explains in his 2017 book *Life 3.0: Being Human in the Time of Artificial Intelligence* that "if we manage to get our self-

---

105   Nick Bostrom, "The Transhumanist FAQ: A General Introduction," 2003, https://www.nickbostrom.com/views/transhumanist.pdf.

improving AI to become friendly by learning and adopting our goals, then we're all set, because we're guaranteed that it will try its best to remain friendly forever."[106]

Tegmark continues as if writing about a human: "For an AI, the subgoal of optimizing its hardware favors both better use of current resources (for sensors, actuators, computation, and so on) and acquisition of more resources. It also implies a desire for self-preservation, since destruction/shutdown would be the ultimate hardware degradation. ...In summary, we can't dismiss 'alpha-male' subgoals such as self-preservation and resource acquisition as relevant only to evolved organisms."[107]

However, although the notion of achieving security via AI safety and friendly AI sounds good on a basic level, it has flaws. Big ones. Think about humans: don't their goals and actions change numerous times during their lifetime? Wouldn't the same be true of superintelligence agents? Besides superintelligence, think about goals and values that well-intentioned humans program into humanoids. If left alone, radically enhanced ones could be further programmed, or they could self-program with choice-making abilities. They could then dismiss humans' desires for ones they prefer.

Apart from those hitches, there are pivotal all-important critical questions, such as whether we can trust research scientists and developers to align themselves with the friendly approach. Why would they want to, considering that their passions, jobs, and careers are on the line? AI development is a worldwide endeavor as is robotics in a more limited way. So, it is likely that determined individuals and perhaps groups can believe it is their right to freely make their own changes concerning superintelligence and humanoid creations. In brief, secure does not mean *absolutely secure.*

---

106   Max Tegmark, *Life 3.0: Being Human in the Time of Artificial Intelligence* (New York: Penguin Random House, 2017), 264.

107   Ibid., 265.

Policy Guidelines on Artificial Ingelligence and Robotics

By the middle of the second century of the twenty-first century considerable activity had begun to take place about the need for oversight and regulation of the development of artificial intelligence. In early 2015, the United Nations Interregional Crime and Justice Research Institute (UNICRI) established a center on AI and robotics to "help focus expertise on Artificial Intelligence (AI) through the UN in a single agency."[108] This center, which opened in September of 2017, focuses on "understanding and addressing the risks and benefits of AI and robotics from the perspective of crime and security through awareness-raising, education, exchange of information, and harmonization of stakeholders."[109] A major emphasis is the importance of retaining human control over weapons systems and the use of force.

These guidelines are significant because the principles have managed to unite nations at a time when there is little international cooperation, and to reinforce the importance of values in AI and robotics development that promote them to be innovative and trustworthy, and has respect for human rights and democratic values.

108　AI Policy – United Nations, Future of Life Institute, https://futureoflife.org/ai-policy-united-nations/ (last visited January 4, 2019), archived at https://perma.cc/9CZ2-ETNX.

109　Centre on Artificial Intelligence and Robotics, UNICRI, para. 5, n.d., http://www.unicri.it/topics/ai_robotics/centre/ (last visited Dec. 10, 2018), archived at https://perma.cc/475Y-ZZ6N.

PROGNOSTICATIONS ON OUR AI AND ROBOTICS FUTURE

As I conducted my research, I realized the public has little knowledge of, or wherewithal to demand, *freedom from* risky AI and robotic developments that loom on the near horizon. At that point, I became upset, because some things are just morally wrong. That was when I decided to take on the task of writing about who and what is behind such developments. Think about this. In the words of Max Tegmark, "Will we control intelligent machines or will they control us? Will intelligent machines replace us, coexist with us, or merge with us? What will it mean to be human in the age of humanoids? What would you like it to mean, and how can we make the future that way?"[110]

Warp speed artificial intelligence creations and robotics have led to a number of books on superintelligence and other aspects of AI and robotics in the mid-term and far-out future. In addition to Max Tegmark's book *Life 3.0*, let's take advantage of several well-known authors on technology for their views on the impact AI could have on humankind. There is Robin Hanson, author of the 2016 book *The Age of Em: Work, Love and Life When Robots Rule the Earth*, who projected that one day, the first truly smart robots, which he calls Ems, will be brain-emulation robots that may rule the world. The concept of Ems reveals how strange humans' descendants may be if there are no controls and bans on humanoid, superintelligence, and other AI development. It also demands critical thinking about common assumptions regarding humanity's moral progress and what we hold dear.

Futurist Yuval Noah Harari, an ancient history specialist, did not participate at the Asilomar conference. Instead, he

110   Tegmark, *Life 3.0*, 38.

followed in the footsteps of other prophet-like long-term authors when he opined in his 2018 book, *21 Lessons for the 21st Century*, that by 2050, unenhanced humans will have become completely useless. Harari is convinced that, simultaneously, AI creations (which I suppose could include robots and humanoids) will take the place of humans. That setting will leave them with vast leisure to happily enjoy their lives.

On a technical level, Adam Piore. in his 2017 book *The Body Builders: Inside the Science of the Engineered Human*, explores the current revolution in human augmentation, taking us into the field of bioengineering and introducing us to the people at its center. Piore argues that the new scientific frontier is the human body and that the greatest engineers of our generations have turned their sights inward and are beginning to revolutionize mankind. His viewpoint, akin to that of transhumanists, those that advocate transhumanism. Transhumanists emphasize that while humans and individual's matter, that by promoting rational thinking and rational means the human organism can be improved. They argue that technological means can be used beyond traditional humanistic methods to eventually enable humans to move beyond what some would think of as "human." In effect, that this revolution is helping humankind to triumph over the limitations and constraints long accepted as an inevitable part of being human.

On the practical current public policy side is Martin Ford, a futurist who focuses on the impact of AI and robotics on society and the economy. He presents a strong argument in his 2016 book, *Rise of the Robots: Technology and the Threat of a Jobless Future*, that advances in robotics and artificial intelligence would eventually make a large fraction of the human workforce obsolete.

Ford's thoughts cannot be taken lightly. They demand serious consideration of the existential risk involved—a risk that cannot be undone, one that poses permanent and significant negative consequences for humanity. The hardcore reason is that creation of friendly AI and superintelligence is a risk-taking venture because humans will depend on the friendliness both of creators of superintelligence and of the machine creations.

Now, a bottom-line, critical issue: Most futurists, and a large portion of the public and scientists, *presume* that radical humanoid and AI development is inevitable, just as change is inevitable. But is it? I argue no, and later in this book I will reveal how controls can be justified and utilized.

Here is a dilemma. Are ordinary citizens really prepared and of sound enough mind to decide on our destiny? Is our populace ready to let the system potentially bring a sort of Armageddon on the world's peoples? Will the "system" fail our citizens?

Beneficial and Moral Consequences of Artificial Intelligence and Robotics

Are you aware that AI innovation is now on the cusp of creating "virtual agents" to multitask, and make judgments and decisions on the pervasiveness of selling personal data? Or that sometime around the mid-2030s some humanoids will be programmed as virtual agents to make decisions without explicit approval of humans? That implants, often as small as an aspirin, use thin metal electrodes to 'listen' to brain activity and essentially 'listen' to your brain activity and then 'talk' directly to your brain?

How about other scientists working furiously to make it possible for human beings to achieve greatly extended life spans? If these wonders are new to you, don't feel alone. That the goal to lengthen life span is not just pie-in-the-sky thinking? As incredible as it may seem there are records of people who have lived to 150 years or more. Can you imagine how older women and men will look less aged, with age differences of as much as 50 or 90 years between spouses and partners?

Positives and Negatives
of AI and Robotics

A fascinating story is that the first artificial neural network (ANN) was invented in 1958 by psychologist Frank Rosenblatt. Called Perceptron, it was intended to model how the human brain processed visual data and learned to recognize objects. Other researchers have since used similar ANNs to study human cognition. Eventually, someone realized that in addition to providing insights into the functionality of the human brain, ANNs could be useful tools in their own right. Their pattern-matching and learning capabilities allowed them to address many problems that were difficult or impossible to solve by standard computational and statistical methods. By the late 1980s, many real-world institutes were using ANNs for a variety of purposes.[111]

Geoffrey Hinton, computer-science professor at the University of Toronto, doubled down in 2012 on his pursuit of the technological idea termed neural network. A neural network is a complex mathematical system, modeled on the web of neurons in the human brain, that can learn discrete tasks by analyzing vast amounts of data. He and two other artificial intelligence pioneering colleagues, Yann Lecun and Yoshua Bengio received the Turing Award, tech's 'Nobel Prize' on March 27, 2019, for the AI research and development that promises to leave no industry unchanged.

As always along the path taken on AI and robotic development, there are both economic benefits and moral consequences. "One thing is very clear, the techniques that we developed can be used for an enormous amount of good

---

111   Alexx Kay, Artificial Neural Networking, Computerworld, February 12, 2001.

affecting hundreds of millions of people," Hinton said.[112] However, he also revealed that while the AI revolution is raising promises computers will make most people's lives more convenient and enjoyable, there are fears that humanity will eventually be living at the mercy of machines. "Bengio, Hinton and Lecun share some of those concerns, especially the doomsday scenarios that envision AI technology developed into weapons systems that wipe out humanity. But the three are far more optimistic about other prospects of AI. Empowering computers to deliver more accurate warnings about floods, and earthquakes, for instance, or detecting health risks, such as cancer and heart attacks, far earlier than human doctors."[113]

As an economist, what I wonder about is the cost/benefit ratio of the above safety-oriented benefits above versus the cost of an AI fomented posthuman condition. But that's getting ahead of our topic at hand. In the near term, AI and robotics are central to how our future might play out in positive and deleterious ways. Scientists and technology developers will get to the next level in which so-called self-supervised AI and humanoid robots will learn to grapple with the unfamiliar. That will lead to aspects of human-like intelligence to the extent AI and humanoids will have the ability to manage virtually all the data about us, even to command and control how our minds work.

<hr>

112   Cade Metz, "Artificial intelligence pioneers win Turing Award—tech's 'Nobel Prize,'" *The Seattle Times*, March 27, 2019. https://www.seattletimes.com/business/artificial-intelligence-pioneers-win-techs-nobel-prize/

113   Ibid.

Neural Implants will Enable Creation of Cyborgs with Superior Capacities

Kevin Kelly, who helped launch *Wired* in 1993 and has served as its executive editor, defines technology as anything a mind produces. He argues we are entering what he has termed the Technium, a network of different supporting technologies, all working together to support each other, that operates as if it is a sentient being. Kelly further believes that "the system is going to be increasingly complex, for there's going to be more minds and artificial minds everywhere. These are all some of the things that I would say technology wants because the system itself is biased in these directions, inherently outside of what humans like us want…in the future when we have robots and AIs, the inventions that these minds make will also be technologies. That's what technology is."[114]

The branch of science known as bionics is the application of biological methods and systems found in nature to the study and design of engineering systems and modern technology. Research on it cuts across a variety of fields such as computer science, engineering, and chemistry, and thus different designations are used. However, over all, bionics has come to mean the merging of organisms and machines, which is essentially the transfer of technology between engineered forms and life forms. One physical result, referred to as a cyborg is cybernetic organism. That term popularly refers to a human with bionic or robotic enhanced abilities, like the ones in the 1970s TV series, *The Bionic Woman* and *The Six Million Dollar Man*. Cyborgs are not to be confused with humanoids, which are robots based on the general structure of humans.

---

114   Kevin Kelly, "The Technium," Edge.org, February 3, 2014. http://edge.org/print/node/25549. See also Kevin Kelly, What Technology Wants (New York: Penguin Group, 2010.)

A natural question is when is a cyborg not a cyborg? Does it really matter? Or is it sufficient to say you know a cyborg when you see one? Actually, recognition of a human cyborg just like robots, humanoid robots and humanoids is not simple. This question is not frivolous, because a strict definition is that cyborgs also have enhancements on human's normal capacities. In addition, some definitions also include that there be metaphysical and physical attachments within or on humans or humanoids. All-in-all, few realize those fitted with devices to at least partially restore vision, pacemakers, prostheses, and have had knee or hip replacement surgery, are technically cyborgs. I admit I am technically a cyborg, as much as I dislike the moniker, because I have had cataract surgery and use hearing aids.

The development of neural implants to increase people's memory is enabling the creation of cyborgs with superior capacities. Since 2015, there have been practices in which installation of neural (relating to a nerve or the nervous system) implants has become relatively simple and fast. A hole is drilled in the skull and the device placed on the surface of the brain. The implants, often as small as an aspirin, "use thin metal electrodes to 'listen' to brain activity and in some cases to stimulate activity in the brain. Attuned to the activity between neurons, a neural implant can essentially 'listen' to your brain activity and then 'talk' directly to your brain."[115] The implants can embody deep brain stimulation to treat serious conditions such as Parkinson's disease and, when stimulation is associated with neurons, would also be able to help the brain to learn faster.

The brain-computer interface is being advanced by several companies. In July, 2019, Elon Musk and top-level scientists from his neuroscience startup, Neuralink, announced a next generation brain-computer interface that would connect human brains and machines with more precision than other devices. The objective is to use the platform to treat neurological conditions like movement disorders, spinal-cord injury, and blindness. The goal of his and other developers is to access as many neurons as possible because that would give scientists more precise reads on activity that underpins brain functions

---

115   Daniel H. Wilson, "Bionic Brains and Beyond," *The Wall Street Journal*, June 1, 2012. http://www.wsj.com/articles/SB100014240527023 0364010457743660122792392

like walking, mood, and speech. The neural recordings are turned into electrical signals that can be fed into a robotic device or back into the nervous system to produce movement or vision.[116]

The time has come when neural implants can strengthen pathways associated with physical tasks. Malcom Gay, author of *The Brain Electric,* explained that managed research efforts by the legendary Defense Advanced Research Projects Agency (DARPA) led to development of a bionic arm using neural implants. The feedback system allowed the arm to communicate directly with the brain to the extent a blindfolded user could identify with 100% accuracy which mechanical fingertips were touched.[117] Think about humanoid robots.

Daniel Watson wrote about neural implants, also called brain implants, that promise mental augmentation: "In the future, it will be feasible for an implant to recognize almost anything. For instance, it could detect inattention. In response, the implant could stimulate the brain toward a state of focused attention…. In an elective setting, a user with this type implant could potentially choose to stay focused on command, while constantly strengthening circuits of the brain associated with concentration."[118] In addition to prosthetic legs and arms enabled by neural implants, Embontic Technology has developed a robotic hand that mimics (biometric) an actual hand. These robotic hands have a "wide variety of potential applications, including robotic manipulation research, medical education and space exploration. It could be adopted as part of an advanced prosthetic, for rescue and military applications."[119] In brief, and undeniably, this technology has copious uses in robot and humanoid robot development.

---

116   Daniela Hernandez and Heather Mack, "Elon Musk's Neuralink Shows Off Advances to Brain-Computer Interface, The Wall Street Journal, July 17, 2019. https://www.wsj.com/articles/elon-musks-neuralink-advances-brain-computer-interface-11563334987

117   Barry Werth, "An Armless Man Raises His Hand," *The Wall Street Journal*, November 18, 2015. http://www.wsj.com/articles/an-armless-man-raises-his-hand-1447803110

118   Ibid.

119   Katherine Long, "New brain implant a reach forward toward UW medical breakthroughs," *The Seattle Times*, February 6, 2018. https://www.seattletimes.com/seattle-news/education/brain-implanted-devices-could-lead-to-uw-medical-breakthroughs/

The Emergence of Mind Control

The most prevalent and recognized form of mind control is through deep brain stimulation. Holes are drilled in the brain and inserted with powerful electrodes to treat a wide range of disorders. These range from Parkinson's disease to epilepsy, bipolar disorder, and multiple sclerosis. On the face of it, deep brain stimulation is a significant step forward from the Post WWII shock treatments and lobotomies that tragically caused great destruction on patients suffering from a variety of psychological disorders.

One opinion by scientists is the notion that with neural implants and other technologies, intelligence, a central property of humans, can be described so precisely that brains intelligence can be simulated by machines. Naturally, that leads to ethical and other philosophical issues because one primary aim in AI is to recreate the capabilities of the human mind. The original notion of mind control, also known as brainwashing or thought control, is now being researched as a way to manipulate or subvert an individual's thinking, behavior, emotions, and decisions by outside sources.

Researchers have now taken a step to computerize people by outfitting them with electronic devices that interact with other devices or people. A strong feature is that the device could operate via voice commands. It seems reasonable that activities using implants such as chips to interact via mind control will be hard to resist. Here's a thought. If mind control can take place between a human and a prosthetic, how about between two humans, a human and a humanoid robot, and between two humanoids? How about group thought?

All of this sounds mundane and beneficial. However, there is a dark side to scientists being able to develop anything they want to as Jaron Lanier, christened the father of virtual reality, points out about behavior modifications in humans.[120] His concerns, which he terms Behavior Modification Empires, go beyond machines and robots to AI and other top-down control schemes. One of his worries is about nefarious results from unintended consequences of algorithm use. Another in his big picture perturbances is that scientists, most of whom are well meaning individuals, will go over the edge.

There are radicals bent on augmenting humans as well as humanoids to the point at which they have the capacity to outperform the best human brains in every field. Nevertheless, one can't help but imagine some humanoids endowed with these mind control technologies by the middle 2030s or sooner. The down side is controls and possibly bans on programming to prevent development of radically enhanced humanoids. My message is beware of complacency.

---

120   Jason Lanier, Dawn of the New Everything: Encounters with Reality and Virtual Reality, Henry Holt and Company, 2017.

BRAINS AND THE DEBATE
ABOUT MIND CHANGE

Raymond Tallis has cogently and succinctly drawn attention to the debate about neuroplasticity, the extraordinary ability of the brain to rewire itself in response to experience, training, injury, and rehabilitation to change the way the brain functions.[121] I bring the debate up about neuroplasticity because of the implications for those fascinated with a posthuman and humanoids world. Tallis focused on the dichotomy between two books. One, *Mind Change* by Susan Greenfield[122] is, in his words, "a nearly panic-stricken assessment of what digital technologies might be doing to our brains."

Mr. Tallis is especially exercised about Greenfield's focus on young people she terms Digital Natives, who have not known life without the Internet. She fears they are being pixelated by hours spent in front of ubiquitous screens, surfing the Internet, social networking, emailing, texting, sharing Instagram posts and tweeting. Tallis disparages her work as lacking scientific vigor. I, on the other hand, laud her insights as I strongly believe that this 'pixelating' does not bode well for the future where the younger generation of Z-ers and Post-Zers may have to vote to save humankind.

Tallis contrasts Ms. Greenfield's "blackly pessimistic" view with Norman Doidge's "wildly optimistic" view in his book, *The Brain's Way of Healing,* in which he has developed his

---

121   Raymond Tallis, "Brainstorms Brewing," The Wall Street Journal, February 27, 2015. http://www.wsj.com/articles/book-review-mind-change-by-susan-greenfield-the-brains-way-of-healing-by-norman-doidge-1425071741

122   Susan Greenfield, *Mind Change*, (New York: Random House, February, 2015).

analysis of the brain and its indications of neuroplasticity. [123] Doidge argues the brain "is 'neuroplastic,' its circuits constantly changing as we move through the world."[124] The important point of his analysis is that the brain is not like hardware in which if you use it, you lose it, because it wears out. Rather, the mainstream view in neuroscience and medicine today on the living brain is "use it or lose it." But there is more.

One aim promoted by singularitarians (a movement defined by the belief that and transhumanists, is to provide a permanent backup to a human's mind-file. The reason is they believe that is how they can become immortal. Singularitarianism is a movement defined by the belief that a technological singularity, (a brain-computer interface that will have progressed to the point of a greater-than-human intelligence from superintelligence development), will likely happen in the near future. Thus, deliberate action ought to be taken to ensure that event benefits humans. Their method is to create one or more non-biological functional copies and then uploading them through the method of whole brain emulation (WBE).

Mind uploading or brain uploading is a popular term for a process by which the mind is transferred from its original biological brain to an artificial computational substrate. This includes a collection of memories, personality, and attributes of a specific individual. The hypothetical process is by copying it to a computer. The computer then runs a simulation model of the brain's information, processing it in a way that it responds in essentially the same way as the original brain. Mind uploading can be accomplished by two methods. One is copy-and-transfer, or gradual replacement of neurons. The other is that the simulated mind could reside in a computer that is inside or connected to a biological body in real life. Added to that, the simulated mind could even be transferred to a robot or a humanoid. Many believe it is humanity's better option than cryonics for preserving the identity of the species.

While complete brain uploading is still speculative, many of the techniques and technologies needed to achieve mind

---

123   Norman Doidge, *The Brain's Way of Healing*, (New York: Viking, 2015).

124   Norman Doidge, "Brain, Heal Thyself," *The Wall Street Journal*, February 6, 2015. http://www.wsj.com/articles/SB2016776107641484369 2504580443981315539578

uploading already exist or are currently under development. Dr. Graziano, a professor at Princeton University pointed out in latter 2019 that "The most widely optimistic projections place mind uploading within a few decades, but I would not be surprised if it took centuries.... However long the technology takes, it seems likely to be a part of our future, so it is worth taking a moment now to think about the implications. What will mind uploading mean for us philosophically and morally?"[125]

So, now a critical moral question: should scientists have a right to actively develop ever more sophisticated uploading procedures when they are fully aware that copying the brain will lead to the existential risk of posthumanity? Tom Harris explains that for some roboticists the ultimate goal of designing robots is to understand how natural intelligence works. "Others envision a world where we live side by side with intelligent machines and use a variety of lesser robots for manual labor, healthcare, and communication. A number of robotics experts predict that robotic evolution will eventually turn us into cyborgs—humans integrated with machines. Conceivably, people in the future could load their minds into a sturdy robot and live for thousands of years!"[126] Is this the kind of world you want for your children and those around the globe?

---

125   Michael S.A. Graziano, "Will your Uploaded Mind Still Be You?" *The Wall Street Journal*, September 14-15, 2019.

126   Tom Harris "How Robots Work" https://science.howstuffworks.com/robot.htm> 11 June 2018

TRUST IN THE SCIENTIFIC COMMUNITY

One researcher has forged a consensus on the need for AI researchers to work on research to be sure the inevitable superintelligence does not stray from programming and orders of its human masters. Integral to it is the concept of friendly AI that would supposedly have a significant positive effect on humanity. But can we trust all in the scientific community to align themselves with the friendly approach? Research scientists and developers value freedom to carry out their desires. Failure to carry out certain aspects of superintelligence herald atrocious consequences. One is singularity, when human biological enhancement, or brain-computer interfaces will have progressed to the point of a greater-than-human intelligence. At that time, the world will enter the era termed post-singularity, at which point there will be no distinction between human and machine. AI and robotics development are world endeavors. Further AI and robotic creations are not just carried out by a small, well-closeted group of researchers who all think alike. Rogues abound.

PART IV

Humankind and Humanoids' Situation in a Posthuman World

"I believe Transhumanism is mankind's only hope for long-term survival," Zobrist preaches, pulling, pulling aside his shirt and showing them all the *H+* tattoo inscribed on his shoulder. "As you can see, I'm fully committed."

"I'm afraid it's only going to get murkier," Sinskey said. "We're on the verge of new technologies that we can't even imagine...." "And new philosophies as well," Sienna added. "The Transhumanist movement is about to explode from the shadows into the mainstream. One of its fundamental tenets is that we as humans have a moral obligation to *participate* in our evolutionary process... to use our technologies to advance the species, to create better humans—healthier, stronger, with higher-functioning brains. Everything will be possible."

—Dan Brown, *Inferno* (2013)

Transhumanist philosophies

The terms and philosophies used in the transhumanist movement are confusing, and interpretations by the media can lead to a number of quite differing views on transhumanism's aspirations. The following explanations are from Version 2.1 *The Transhumanist FAQ: A General Introduction.*[127] Quotes are followed by the *FAQ* page number in parentheses. It is uncanny how the largest part of transhumanist aspirations and agenda mostly also apply to radically enhanced humanoids. I take the liberty of adding the term humanoid in parentheses and italics in the following text to indicate where the transhumanist term can be applied to radically enhanced humanoids.

127   Nick Bostrom, *The Transhumanist FAQ: A General Introduction, Version 2.1* (2003). http://www.tranhumanism.org/resources/FAQv21.pdf.

"Transhumanism"

"To a transhumanist progress occurs when more people (*humanoids*) can become able to transform their lives, and the ways they relate to others, in accordance with their deepest values…. Transhumanists seek to create a world in which autonomous individuals (*humanoids*) may choose to remain unenhanced or choose to be enhanced and in which these choices will be respected." (4).

"On the dark side of the spectrum, transhumanists recognize that some of these coming technologies could potentially cause great harm to human life; even the survival of our species could be at risk. Seeking to understand the dangers and working to prevent disasters is an essential part of the transhumanist agenda." (5).

"POSTHUMAN"
(POSTHUMAN CONDITION)

"It is sometimes useful to talk about possible future beings (humanoids) whose basic capacities so radically exceed those of present humans as to be no longer unambiguously human (humanoid) by our current standards. The standard word for such beings is 'posthuman.' (Care must be taken to avoid misinterpretation. 'Posthuman' (posthuman condition) does not denote just anything that happens to come after the human era, nor does it have anything to do with the 'posthumous.' In particular, it does not imply that there are no humans anymore.)

Posthumans (*posthumanoids*) could be completely synthetic artificial intelligences, or they could be enhanced uploads [Uploading, also called 'mind uploading' or 'brain reconstruction' is the process of transferring an intellect from a biological brain to a computer], or they could be the result of making many smaller but cumulatively profound augmentations to a biological human (*advanced humanoid*). The latter alternative would probably require either the redesign of the human (*humanoid*) organism using advanced nanotechnology or its radical enhancement using some combination of technologies such as genetic engineering, psychopharmacology, anti-aging therapies, neural interfaces, advanced information management tools, memory enhancing drugs, wearable computers, and cognitive techniques.

Some authors write as though simply by changing our self-conception, we have become or could become posthuman. This is a confusion or corruption of the original meaning of the term. The changes required to make us posthuman are too profound to be achievable by merely altering some aspect of psychological theory or the way we think about ourselves.

Radical technological modifications to our brains and bodies (*humanoid platforms*) are needed.

It is difficult for us to imagine what it would be like to be a posthuman person (*post humanoid*). Posthumans may have experiences and concerns that we cannot fathom, thoughts that cannot fit into the three-pound lumps of neural tissue that we use for thinking. Some posthumans (*posthumanoids*) may find it advantageous to jettison their bodies altogether and live as information patterns on vast super-fast computer networks. Their minds may be not only be more powerful than ours but may also employ different cognitive architectures or include new sensory modalities that enable greater participation in their virtual reality settings. Posthuman minds might be able to share memories and experiences directly, greatly increasing the efficiency, quality, and modes in which posthumans could communicate with each other. The boundaries between posthuman minds may not be as sharply defined as those between humans.

Posthumans might shape themselves and their environment in so many new and profound ways that speculations about the detailed features of posthumans (posthumanoids) and the posthuman (posthumanoid) world are likely to fail." (5-6).

"Will New Technologies Only Benefit the Rich and Powerful?"

"It is clear that everybody (all *humanoids*) can benefit greatly from improved technology. Initially, however, the greatest advantages will go to those who have the resources, the skills, and the willingness to learn to use new tools. One can speculate that some technologies may cause social inequalities to widen. For example, if some form of intelligence amplification becomes available, it may at first be so expensive that only the wealthiest can afford it. The same could happen when we learn how to genetically enhance our children. Those who are already well off would become smarter and make even more money. This phenomenon is not new. Rich parents send their kids to better schools and provide them with resources such as personal connections and information technology that may not be available to the less privileged. Such advantages lead to greater earnings later in life and serve to increase social inequalities." (20-21).

"Trying to ban technological innovation on these grounds, however, would be misguided. If a society judges existing inequality to be unacceptable, a wiser remedy would be progressive taxation and the provision of community-funded services such as education, IT access in public libraries, genetic enhancements covered by social security, and so forth." (21).

Aren't These Future
Technologies Very Risky?
Could They Even Cause
Our Extinction?

"Yes, and this implies an urgent need to analyze the risks before they materialize and to take steps to reduce them. Biotechnology, nanotechnology, and artificial intelligence pose especially serious risks of accidents and abuse." (21-22).

"One can distinguish between, on the one hand, endurable or limited hazards... and, on the other hand, existential risks – events that would cause the extinction of intelligent life or permanently and drastically cripple its potential.... Transhumanists therefore recognize a moral duty to promote efforts to reduce existential risks. The gravest existential risks facing us in the coming decades will be of our own making. These include: Destructive uses of nanotechnology. The accidental release of a self-replicating nanobot into the environment, where it would proceed to destroy the entire biosphere, is known as the 'gray goo scenario.'" (23).

"No threat to human (*humanoid*) existence is posed by today's AI systems or their near-term successors. But if and when superintelligence is created, it will be of paramount importance that it be endowed with human-friendly values. An imprudently or maliciously designed superintelligence, with goals amounting to indifference or hostility to human welfare, could cause our extinction. Another concern is that the first superintelligence, which may become very powerful because of its superior planning ability and because of the technologies it could swiftly develop, would be built to serve only a single person or a small group (such as its programmers or the corporation that commissioned it). While this scenario may not entail the extinction of literally all intelligent life, it nevertheless constitutes an existential risk because the future that would result would be one in which a great part of humanity's (*humanoids*) potential had been permanently destroyed and in which at most a tiny fraction of all humans (*humanoids*) would get to enjoy the benefits of posthumanity (*Posthumanoid condition*)." (24).

Naïve Mandate: Creatures Should Be Loving and Caring Toward Humankind

The Transhumanist FAQ provides a mandate—a hope actually—that a superintelligence should be loving and caring of humankind (*humanoids*). The rather long but compelling FAQ states "What about the hypothetical case in which someone intends to create, or turn themselves into, a being (humanoid) of so radically enhanced capacities that a single one or a small group of such individuals would be capable of taking over the planet? This is clearly not a situation that is likely to arise in the imminent future, but one can imagine that, perhaps in a few decades, the prospective creation of superintelligent machines could raise this kind of concern." (33-34).

The FAQ continues "The would-be creator of a new life form with such surpassing capabilities would have an obligation to ensure that the proposed being is free from psychopathic tendencies and, more generally, that it has humane inclinations. For example, a superintelligence should be built with a clear goal structure that has friendliness to humans as its top goal. Before running such a program, the builders of a superintelligence should be required to make a strong case that launching it would be safer than alternative courses of action." (33-34).

Here are my thoughts. I argue the transhumanist mandate could sound fine on the surface to some people, because transhumanists make the issue of control over creation of new life forms as a simple friend-to-friend task. However, can we citizens realistically have absolute belief or conviction that developers of technologies will do the right thing to perpetuate humankind as we know it? Can we really expect all of them to make choices that will be in the best interest of all peoples in the world? Can we simply put our faith in researchers, developers, and scientists all over the globe to prioritize the greatest happiness for all?

Our government should play a vital role in decisions made about superintelligence and radically enhanced humanoid development. Sadly, trust in government is at rock bottom. Most troubling is exactly how it will be possible to keep track of all those around the world committed to endowing humans and humanoids with radical enhancements that can lead to posthumanity. Can we simply have confidence that America's and global governments will voluntarily strive to obtain a worldwide agreement to never launch risky superintelligence innovations? If obtained will all parties follow through and enforce compliance of said agreement? I firmly believe it is naïve to think so.

Technologically speaking, creation of radically endowed humans as well as humanoids that can lead to a new subspecies of *Homo sapiens* is not just a silly sci-fi fabrication. Nowadays, it's a new ballgame, as some transhumanist-oriented research-ers and scientists seek to create what is essentially a new spe-cies, where there will be no distinction between human and machine. Considering that, can we boldly ask, aren't the goals of life extension, posthumanity, and mind control forms of eu-genics of both humans and humanoid creatures?

PART V

CHOICE MAKERS OF OUR FUTURE

Life is not a search for experience, but for ourselves. Having discovered our fundamental level we realize that it conforms to our destiny and we find peace.

—Cesare Pavese, *This Business of Living* (1940)

There is one more important aspect that is germane to conditions surrounding the precautionary principle: human rights' role in scientific research and humankind's happiness. As might be expected the scientific research issue is complicated, as Silja Voeneky points out in her chapter, "Human Rights and the Legitimate Governance of Existential and Global Catastrophic Risks" in the 2018 book, *Human Rights, Democracy, and Legitimacy in a World of Disorder.*[128] Apart from her discussion on the existential and global catastrophic risks, she argues that the existing human rights framework has so far been left aside as a (potential) important basis and starting point for a legitimate governance regime.

---

128   Silja Voeneky and Gerald L. Neuman, eds, *Human Rights, Democracy, and Legitimacy in a World of Disorder*, (Cambridge: Cambridge University Press, 2018).

FREEDOM FROM VERSUS FREEDOM TO CARRY OUT RESEARCH

So now a critical question: how about scientists' value of *freedom to* carry out research that can lead to existential and global catastrophic risks? Voeneky explains that freedom of research is not only a justified (i.e., moral or ethical) value, it is also a legally binding human right. That is because there is a shared view that freedom of research is entailed in the right of freedom of thought and freedom of expression in international human rights treaties. For instance, the International Covenant on Civil and Political Rights and the European Convention on Human Rights are two such treaties. But, don't some parties also have *freedom from* those scientists' research?

The answer is yes, as she goes on to write, "to protect freedom of research as a human right does not mean that this freedom is absolute. According to legal international human rights, the protection of the life and health of human beings are inter alia (among other things) legitimate aims that can justify proportional limitations[129] of the right of freedom of science. The human rights framework therefore stresses that, if states limit the freedom of science for legitimate purposes, it is necessary to find proportional limitations, even if the probability of the realization of an existential and global catastrophic risk is close to zero or cannot be quantified."[130]

---

129   What proportionality means is linked to the risks and benefits on can reasonably anticipate.

130   Ibid, 154, 155.

Human Rights' Role in Scientific Research

Silja Voeneky's thesis is that a legitimate governance regime of existential and global catastrophic risks should be based on human rights, more precisely, legally binding human rights.[131] She refers to legally binding human rights as the premise that human rights are justified in a supra-legal [her term] sense by a deontological theory of normative ethics. The premise holds that at least some acts are morally obligatory regardless of their consequences. They are legally binding human rights that *prima facie* (based on the first impression, accepted as current until proven otherwise) corresponds with moral human rights. She also states that this does not mean that other ethical approaches to solving problems of existential and global catastrophic risks are ruled out not as long as they are compatible with human rights. However, it does mean that she rejects those views that utilitarian arguments (practical, realistic, sensible, down-to-earth) should be the primary standard to measure the legitimacy of a government regime for existential and global catastrophic risks.

Voeneky explains that international treaties "obligate states not only to respect, but also to protect the fundamental rights of individuals…. They state that States parties are obligated by international human rights treaties to take appropriate (legal) measures to protect the life of individuals."[132] In her view, "this duty includes a duty to protect the life of individuals against risk in low or unknown probability scenarios which means that *no actual or direct threat* for a protected right exists—as long as there are risks of an existential or globally catastrophic nature."[133]

---

131   Ibid, 151.

132   Ibid, 155.

133   Ibid, 155-156.

The UN Human Rights Committee's 2017 draft states "the duty to protect the right to life by law also includes an obligation for States parties to take appropriate legal measures in order to protect life from all *foreseeable threats*, including threats emanating from private persons and entities."[134] The 2017 draft comment spells out similarly, later on, that "States parties are thus under a due diligence obligation to undertake reasonable positive measures, which do not impose on them impossible or disproportionate burdens, in *response to foreseeable threats to life* originating from private persons and entities, whose conduct is not attributable to the State."[135]

Silja Voeneky unwittingly sheds light on limitations of the triumvirate's apparent power "It does not seem to be a disproportionate limitation of science or technological progress to lay down a rule that there is a burden of proof for those who fund science (or for scientists) to show that there are more benefits than risks if there is plausibility for an existential or global catastrophic risk."[136] Further, she maintains that because of the global dimension of the risks, it seems more plausible to argue that we need a global consensus to solve the problem of *freedom to*, as well as to determine whether to allow or prohibit certain experiments or techniques.

The previous explanation makes it clear that while scientists are legally granted the right of freedom of thought and expression, that freedom is not absolute. That, in turn, implies that legitimate concerns can justify proportional limitations on the right of freedom in scientific research and development. In simple terms, that means regulations, controls, and bans can legally be put in place by relevant governmental authorities and other groups. That includes the group's colleagues in the same field of scientific endeavor.

---

134   Ibid, 156.

135   Ibid, 157.

136   Ibid, 161.

Choice for a Posthuman Condition

The UN Human Rights Committee's 2017 draft stresses that the right to life "concerns the entitlement of individuals to be free from acts and omissions intended or expected to cause their unnatural or premature death...." This draft comment holds that the duty to protect the right of society as a whole "implies that States parties must establish a legal framework to ensure the full enjoyment of the right to life by all individuals."[137] To me, the term enjoyment of the right to life in this 2017 draft translates into a social responsibility to protect happiness and quality of life of both humans and humanoids.

We do live in a stressful, rapidly changing new reality. So, what is required to achieve happiness? Evaluation of what makes us happy and how to measure it is of ultimate importance because our future can be a source of happiness or of great sadness, depending on choices made about calamitous coming events. A rhetorical question: would Americans, and humans the world over, be happier, or really care if superintelligence and radically enhanced humanoids directly or indirectly impinged on our lives?

The question of gaining happiness from any kind of artificial intelligence and humanoids is an intriguing one. Transhumanists emphasize that while humans and individual's matter, by promoting rational thinking and rational means, the human organism can be improved. They argue that technological means can be used beyond traditional humanistic methods to eventually enable humans to move beyond what some would think of as "human."[138] Adherents of singularitarianism believe

---

137   Ibid 156.

138   Taken from the Version 2.1, *The Transhumanist FAQ: A General Introduction.*

technological creation of smarter-than-human intelligence to be a watershed moment in history, perhaps more comparable to the rise of *Homo sapiens* than to past breakthroughs in technology.[139] To them, the prospect of superintelligence and technological singularity is not scary—just the opposite, simply a leap to a different and better quality of life.

So, could and would, enhanced' humans in a posthuman condition be happier than when they were not enhanced or were mildly enhanced humans? Would their lives be more meaningful and enjoyable compared to not being enhanced? Do you recall that the posthuman condition is the state following enhancement so extreme some of those individuals would no longer be humans by our current standards?

Let's take a rather extreme example about *purpose* in individual lives and enhancements. Imagine a person only meeting basic and security needs that lacks friendship and love, the third level out of five in Maslow's theory about happiness. That person seems to have no reason for living each day in current unenhanced conditions and finds no *purpose* to current life. Then assume that individual becomes acquainted with transhumanist philosophies and begins to wonder, "Who am I anyway? What do I want out of life? What's wrong with my life now? I don't even seem to have any *purpose* in life. So, why not explore life through radical enhancements, the one that some transhumanists aspire to? It sounds like nirvana. That might be just the ticket."

That individual finally decides, and seeks out and acquires enhancements. Perhaps he or she is truly in a Shangri La life, free from all stress, harmoniously living in that environment, and winds up bouncing from one peak experience to the next. But maybe that endowed person's transformation turns into a perpetual nightmare. What then? Will there be a reversal process for enhancements that would allow a person or a humanoid to regain his or her original brain and personality? Suppose you decide to take the leap. You wind up in a posthuman condition. Your new life is not what you had been promised. Would you wonder with despair how you could have ever hated your pre-enhanced life? Would you feel like a fool, wondering how you ended up alone?

Do you believe in the right for us to control our own destinies? How about the populace being the choice makers

---

139   Paraphrased from page 44, WTA, *The Transhumanist FAQ.*

of our futures? Digging deep, can those engaged in robotics be trusted to make rational choices regarding the necessary action that has to be taken to ban robots, humanoid robots, or humanoids? Unfortunately, there are rogues among citizens and some among those that practice robotics.

Critical questions are in order. Are all of those around the world that create and develop the technologies that will dramatically affect our destinies truly concerned about life satisfaction, quality of life, or whatever else happiness is termed? Will we, the citizens, control intelligent machines or will they control us? What would it mean to be human in an age when humanoids coexist with or replace us?

The story goes on. Rationally, steps must be taken to control development of humanoids by the mid to later 2030s, or whenever these creatures are prognosticated to be on par with humans. The reason? A half dozen years or so later, like in the late 40's. Some would no longer be unambiguously human by our current standards. At that time, some radically enhanced humanoids with free will could feasibly make choices to such a degree that a new species might be created. Likewise, with those developers of AI who are determined to create some form of superintelligence, do they truly believe their efforts will lead to happiness and better living in a much better world? The takeaway: Regulations, controls, or bans must be placed on these two technologies within well-judged prudent times.

Our Future and Happiness

Should the populace be content to relegate our future and happiness to the whims of those in positions of power regarding regulations on superintelligence and radically enhanced humanoids? If not, should citizens fight back, and if so, how? In fact, do a significant even genuinely want to be in control of our lives? At least, to fight for it? Let's face it, the height of arrogance in America, as well as some other countries, is belief by the elite that ordinary citizens cannot be trusted to make properly informed choices about weighty matters such as technology and the world's future.

Unfortunately, at this point, at least trust in Americas government to do the right thing and stand up to the elites is so low that the triumvirate has a clear advantage. So, in reality, what can be done by the citizens to assure appropriate measures are taken at prudent, well-judged times to avoid catastrophes from superintelligence and radical humanoid development?

A CALL TO ACTION

Each new generation wants to explore and feel adventurous. That is natural. The difference from earlier generations shared by many of the two younger sets, the Z Generation born 1997-2012 and the Post-Z-ers, that rapid change is a desirable and constant element in their lives. It is not an exaggeration to argue that the younger generation worships change and views it as a definition of progress. Thus, continual release of new technological creations is high on their list of priorities. What is also clearly discernible is citizens acceptance as normal that technologies also control much of their lives. Another grave downside is many don't realize that the term "progress" is the process of improving or getting nearer to achieving or accomplishing something beneficial for the future of society. But cheer up. Many do find *purpose* in their lives and will fight for the good of humankind. So where does that leave us?

What I have provided is an early warning, an explanation, and evidence about robotic technologies that will affect your life, your children's lives, and the lives of others on this planet. Now dear reader, it is up to you to keep this conversation going. The bottom line on decisions about humanity, as we know it, comes down to three broad choices (1) just let events unfold, (2) submit to the adventure of unfettered humanoid development, or (3) take action to judicially place controls on existential risks detailed in this book. I have my lovely wife, three remarkable children, and friends all over the world with children. I know my choice. I emphatically vote to take action.

GLOSSARY

(Last revision January 8, 2022)

Thanks is given to the multitude of sources I used that include dictionaries, encyclopedias, technical books, Wikipedia, etc., and for references and footnotes in the same. Many of these definitions are open to debate because the technical aspects surrounding them are changing so rapidly. In any event, the definitions are to help a wide swath of the public to understand the topic concerned, not as a definitive collection for technologists.

Actroid – a humanoid robot that looks very much like a real human.

Advanced humanoids – the term is applied to those in two stages. The initial one, in 2030-2035, in which they are moderately augmented and mix with humans, and 2035-2040, in which early advanced ones are generally accepted by humans, and the later part, when many are on par with humans.

Android – a humanoid robot or humanoid created as a synthetic organism designed to look and act as much as possible like a real person. The term popularly used for both males and female robots. The word has roots in androgynous, having the characteristics or nature of both male or female. Technically, an android is the male form. Gynoid is the female form. Droid is an abridgement of android.

Animaloid – a robot created as a synthetic organism designed to look and act as much as possible like a real animal.

Anthropocentric – regarding humankind as the central or most important element of existence, especially as opposed to God or animals. Considering humans and their existence as the most important and central fact about life.

Artificial Insemination – Injection of semen into the vagina or uterus other than by sexual intercourse.

Artificial Intelligence – (Definition 1) machinery with the ability to reason and solve problems. It also refers to the branch of computer science that includes the study and design of intelligence agents, the melding of humans, robots and machines, and aims to create intelligence of machines and robots.

Artificial Intelligence – (Definition 2. Oxford Dictionary) the theory and development of computer systems able to perform tasks normally requiring human intelligence, such as visual perception, speech recognition, decision-making, and translation between languages.

Automaton – a self-operated machine. A moving mechanical device made in imitation of a human being. A machine that operates on its own without the need for human control, or a person who acts like a machine.

Autonomous – capable of acting independently, without outside control. Autonomous machines can determine what actions to take without human direction.

Avatar – an image that represents you on the screen in an online game or chatroom or a person melding their mind and movements with a robot surrogate, or avatar.

Basic Humanoids – those in the basic stage of development. Also, the term used for androids because they have appearance, mobility, vision, and ability to defend themselves and not harm others.

Bio-android – used interchangeably with the term android.

Biological Engineering, also termed biotechnological engineering or bioengineering – an engineering discipline that combines methods and concepts in biology with those of computer sciences, mathematics, physics and chemistry to solve real world life sciences problems by using the engineer's knowledge of complex artificial systems.

Bionics – application of biological method and systems found in nature to the study and design of engineering systems and modern technology. It also has come to include merging organism and machine, also referred to as a cybernetic organism, bionic person, or cyborg.

Bionic brains – artificial brain.

Biorobot – biologically inspired robot.

Biorobotics – the field focused on the construction of biologically inspired or biometric robots.

Bot – a device or piece of software that can execute commands, reply to messages, or perform routine tasks, as online searches, either automatically or with minimal human intervention.

Biotechnology (biotech) – use of living systems and organisms to develop or make useful products. Additionally, it is any technological application that uses biological systems, living organisms, or derivatives thereof, to make or modify products or processes for specific use.

Blastocyst – a structure formed in early development of mammals.

Blastocyte – an undifferentiated embryonic cell.

Brain Emulation (see Whole brain emulation).

Chatbot – computer program that can simulate human conversation. Examples include personal assistants such as Siri and chatbots that answer customers' questions on company websites.

Chimera – single organism composed of cells with distinct genotypes. In animals, this means an individual derived from two or more zygotes, which can include possessing blood cells of different blood types, subtle variations in form (phenotype) and, if the zygotes were of differing sexes, then even the possession of both female and male sex organs.

Cisgenic – the resulting organism when genetic material from the same species, or a species that can naturally breed with the host, is used.

Cloning – the process of producing similar populations of genetically identical individuals that occurs in nature when organisms such as bacteria, insects, plants, or animals reproduce asexually.

Cobot – or co-robot (from collaborative robot) is a robot intended to physically interact with humans in a shared workspace. The term is also used for humanoids that work hand in hand with humans.

Cybernetic human – incorrect usage as a synonym for a humanoid.

Cybernetic organism – commonly known a cyborg, it is essentially the transfer of technology between engineered forms and life forms.

Cyborg – an organism that has enhanced abilities due to augmentations and enhancements, particularly mechanical parts. A stricter definition is enhancing normal capabilities. The general use is for physical attachments within or on humans. For example, a human fitted with prosthetic leg, mechanical parts in knee surgery, pace makers, and hearing aids. In science fiction, a creature that is part human, part machine.

Cyborgization – endowment within or on humans of a metaphysical or physical attachment.

Deep learning – process in which multilayered neural networks are exposed to vast amounts of data. On their own, the networks learn to analyze the data and draw conclusions.

DNA – a molecule composed of two chains that coil around each other to form a double helix carrying the genetic instructions used in the growth, development, functioning, and reproduction of all known living organisms and many viruses.

Droid – abridgement of android.

Embryo transfer – a step in the process of assisted reproduction in which embryos are placed into the uterus of a female with the intent to establish a pregnancy.

Enhanced humans – see Human enhancement.

Existential Risk – a risk that cannot be undone that poses permanent large negative consequences to humanity.

Exoskeleton – an outer framework worn by a person that may be powered to assist the wearer in boosting strength and endurance. A rigid external covering for the body in some invertebrate animals, especially arthropods.

Expert systems – computers that store vast amounts of information about a specific field, such as business medicine. Expert systems are also programmed with detailed rules about how to process the data.

Extropianism – a philosophy of or belief in an evolving framework of values and standards for continually improving the human condition.

Facultative – In biology, it means organisms that can live with another organism, but do not have to. In contrast, some organisms are obligate, meaning they depend on another for survival.

Gamete – a haploid (term used when a cell has half the usual number of chromosomes) cell that fuses with another haploid cell during fertilization (conception) in organisms that sexually reproduce.

Genetic engineering (GE) – also called gene modification, it is the direct manipulation of an organism using biotechnology methods to alter the genetic makeup of an organism.

Genoid – the female form of an android. Technically, android is the male form.

Genetically modified organism (GMO) – an organism generated through genetic engineering.

Genomics – the field within the discipline of genetics that focuses on determination and analysis of the structure of genomes (the complete set of DNA within a single cell of an organism such as humans). It also includes efforts to determine the entire DNA sequence of organisms and to map them.

Hominoids – a primate of a group that includes humans, their fossil ancestors, and the anthropoid apes.

Homo sapiens – the kind of species of human being that exists now.

Humans – member of the species Homo sapiens; a human being, especially a person as distinguished from an animal or (in science fiction) an alien. Humans are multicellular organisms.

Human enhancement – attempts to temporarily or permanently overcome current limitations of the human body by the use of technological means to select or alter human characteristics and capacities whether or not the alterations result in bringing about characteristics and capacities that lie beyond the existing human range.

Humanoid – a robot based on the general structure of a human. Also, the term generally used in place of android or humanoid robot in an effort to humanize the mechanical being and make it more acceptable, and in many cases, loveable. In science fiction, the term humanoid is most commonly used to refer to alien beings with a body plan that is generally like that of a human, including upright stance and bipedalism.

Humanoid robot – a mechanical or artificial device more robot than humanoid in the basic stages leading to the advanced humanoid stage.

Humanoids, Advanced – see Advanced humanoids.

Humanoids, Basic – see Basic humanoids.

Humanoids, radically enhanced – see Radically Enhanced Humanoids

Humanity+ – Humanity Plus is an international organization derived from rebranding to project a more humane image from The World Transhumanist Association (WTA), which advocates the ethical use of emerging technologies to enhance human capacities.

Humanoidization – the process of developing robots through symbiosis with humans to the extent advanced humanoids are common and on par with humans.

Humanoidization, Radical – the process of humanoids attaining such radically advanced capacities that they would no longer be unambiguously human by our current standards.

In vitro fertilization – the process of fertilization by extracting eggs, retrieving a sperm sample, and then manually combining an egg and sperm in a laboratory dish. The embryo(s) is then transferred to the uterus.

Intelligence – Following are uses of this term connected with superintelligence[140]

Friendly AI – superintelligence whose goals are aligned with ours. Alternative: friendly artificial intelligence (also friendly AI or FAI) is a hypothetical artificial general intelligence (AGI) that would have a positive (benign) effect on humanity. It is a part of the ethics of artificial intelligence and is closely related to machine ethics.

Whereas machine ethics is concerned with how an artificially intelligent agent should behave, friendly artificial intelligence research is focused on how to practically bring about this behaviour and ensuring it is adequately constrained.

Artificial General Intelligence (AGI) – the ability to accomplish any cognitive task at least as well as humans. Alternative: the hypothetical intelligence of a machine that has the capacity to understand or learn any intellectual task that a human being can.

General Intelligence – ability to accomplish virtually any goal, including learning.

Intelligence – the ability to accomplish complex goals.

Intelligence explosion – recursive self-improvement rapidly leading to superintelligence.

---

140   Taken from Max Tegmark, *Life 3.0: Being Human in the Time of Artificial Intelligence* (New York: Knopf, 2017), 39, and Stephanie Sammartino McPherson, *Artificial Intelligence: Building Smarter Machines* (Minneapolis: Twenty-first Century Books, 2018), 97.

Narrow Intelligence – the ability to accomplish a narrow set of goals, e.g., play chess or drive a car.

Singularity – intelligence explosion.

Strong AI – AGI.

Superintelligence – general intelligence far beyond human level.

Synthetic intelligence – an alternative term for artificial intelligence which emphasizes that the intelligence of machines need not be an imitation or in any way artificial; it can be a genuine form of intelligence.

Universal intelligence – ability to acquire general intelligence given access to data and resources.

Knockout organism – the result when genetic material is removed from the target organism. Knockouts are used to study gene function, usually by investigating the effect of gene loss.

Law of Accelerating Returns – theory by Ray Kurzweil that electronic development, such as improvement in the speed, memory, and power of computers, proceeds at a rate that is continuously doubling.

Life – a principle or force that is considered to underlie the distinctive quality of animate beings, a process that can retain its complexity and replicate.

Machine ethics – the concern with how an artificially intelligent agent should behave. See also: Friendly AI.

Mind control – originally known as brain washing or thought control, it is increasingly being researched a way to manipulate or subvert an individual's thinking, behavior, emotions or decision by outside sources. The most prevalent and recognized form of mind control is through deep brain stimulation by drilling holes in the brain and inserting powerful electrodes to treat a wide range of disorders. Another form termed mind control is a technique that allows humans to interact with their surroundings through so-called avatars.

Nanobots – tiny robots made of DNA that can walk, pivot, and even work with microscopic forklifts.

Nanotechnology – the production and use of machines that are only slightly larger than atoms and molecules. Some researchers believe AI will combine with nanotechnology to transform medicine and other disciplines.

Neural nets – computer systems that loosely mimic the workings of the human brain.

Neuroscience – science of the nervous system, traditionally seen as a branch of biology, which now covers a multitude of other fields and is an integral part of Artificial Intelligence.

Nucleotide – the basic structural unit of nucleic acids such as DNA

Obligate – In biology, some organisms are obligate, meaning they depend on another for survival. Others are termed facultative, meaning they can live with another organism, but do not have to.

Organism – a living thing, it is the smallest contiguous unit of life.

Pharmacogenomics – studies of how a person's genetic makeup affects his or her body's response to drugs.

Pharming – a combination of farming and pharmaceutical refers to the use of genetic engineering to insert genes into host animals or plants that would otherwise not express those genes, thus creating a genetically modified organism (GMO).

Plutocracy – formally, government by the wealthy. In more general parlance, it is any form of government in which the wealthy exercise the preponderance of power, whether it is direct or indirect.

Plutocrat – a person who is powerful because of their wealth.

Posthuman – possible future beings whose basic capacities so radically exceed those of present humans, as to be no longer unambiguously human by our current standards.

Posthuman condition – state following enhancement so extreme some individuals would no longer be humans by our current standards and could choose to overcome humans, leaving at most, a tiny fraction of all humans to enjoy the benefits of posthumanity.

Posthumanoid condition – state following radical humanoidization in which some humanoids would no longer be on par with humans by our current standards and choose to overcome humans leaving at most a tiny fraction of all humans to enjoy the benefits of humanity as they know it and/or a posthuman condition.

Posthumanism – a term not used by transhumanists, but sometimes incorrectly used as a synonym for transhumanism.

Posthumanity – the result from creation of superintelligence that, while it may not entail the extinction of literally all intelligent life, it nevertheless constitutes an existential risk because the future that would result would be one in which a great part of humanity's potential had been permanently destroyed.

Posthumanoid – possible future beings whose basic capacities so radically exceed those of advanced humanoids, as to be no longer unambiguously humanoids by our current standards.

Post-singularity – the point beyond which there is no distinction between human and machine.

Radically enhanced humans – those with advanced capacities that they would no longer be unambiguously human by our current standards.

Radically enhanced humanoids – those in the radically advanced stage of development or beyond with such radically advanced capacities that they exceed those of present humans. At that point, advanced humanoids would no longer be unambiguously human by our current standards.

Recombinant DNA (rDNA) – molecules that are DNA sequences derived by molecular cloning methods that create new DNA sequences that would not otherwise be found in the genome.

Robot – a mechanical or artificial device primarily guided by a computer program or some electronic method.

Robot, Advanced – robots accepted by humans for their workplace and society because they have appearance, mobility, and other useful attributes.

Robot, Autonomous – stand-alone system, complete with its own computer termed the controller. The most advanced example is the smart robot.

Robots, Basic – the term I use for robots that have the most elemental attributes as machines. Synonym for humanoid robot.

Robots, Fourth Generation – in the research and development phase that includes artificial intelligence, self-replication, self-assembly, and nanoscale size.

Robot, Smart – stand-alone robot, which has a built-in AI system that can learn from its environment and experience to build on those capabilities and knowledge.

Robots, Swarm – work in fleets with all members under the supervision of a single controller.

Robots, Telepresence – simulate the experience and some of the capabilities of being present. Examples are home monitoring, smart houses, remote business consultations, and many other possibilities.

Roboethics – the area of study concerned with what rules should be created for robots to ensure their ethical behavior and how to design ethical robots.

Roboethical standards – ones related to rights of robots and interactions with humans.

Robotics – the branch of technology that deals with the design, construction, operation, and application of robots.

Robotoid – an artificial lifeform created through processes that are totally different from cloning or synthetics. Also, a small robot, child sized or smaller.

Robot fetishism – the fetishistic attraction to humanoid robots. It also refers to people acting like robots or dressed in robot costumes.

Sapience – the quality of being wise, or wisdom.

Sapient – a human of the species.

Sentient – capable of thinking and feeling; being aware of one's existence.

Sexbots – humanoids developed for personal sexual satisfaction or as sex workers in commercial establishments.

Singularity – also known as technological singularity. See technological singularity.

Singularitarianism – a movement defined by the belief that a technological singularity—the creation of superintelligence—will likely happen in the near future, and that deliberate action ought to be taken to ensure that the singularity benefits humans.

Species – group of individuals that actually or potentially interbreed in nature and is the biggest gene pool possible under natural conditions.

Social robotics – study of how robots, humanoids and humans learn to relate to each other.

Somatic cells – any cell of a living organism other than the reproductive cells.

Sophont – An intelligent being; a being with a base reasoning capacity roughly equivalent to or greater than that of a human being. The word does not apply to machines unless they have true artificial intelligence, rather than mere processing capacity.

Superintelligence – Any intellect that greatly exceeds the cognitive performance of humans in virtually all domains of interest.

Symbiont – an organism living in a state of symbiosis or in a symbiotic relationship.

Symbiote – synonym for symbiont.

Symbiosis – commonly defined as a relationship between people, companies, etc. that is to the advantage of both. A generally accepted definition in biology is the living together of unlike organisms, which has been broadened to cover all species.

Synthetic Biology – an interdisciplinary branch of biology that combines disciplines such as biotechnology, evolutionary biology, molecular biology, systems biology, biophysics, computer engineering, and genetic engineering.

Technium – a network of different technologies all working together to support each other that operates as if it is a sentient being.

Technocentrism – a term that denotes a value system centered on technology and its ability to control and protect the environment.

Technocracy – a social or political system in which people with scientific knowledge have a lot of power; a sense of being governed primarily by technical experts; a meritocracy composed of those with power derived from scientific knowledge.

Technocrat – a term for a member of a powerful technical elite or someone who advocates the supremacy of technical experts; an expert in science, engineering, etc. who has a lot of power in politics and/or industry; those that have inordinate power and control through technology over society.

Technium – Kevin Kelly's term for a network of different supporting technologies all working together to support each other that operates as if it is a sentient being.

Technological singularity – the theoretical emergence of superintelligence through technological means. A hypothetical moment when artificial intelligence, human biological enhancement, or brain-computer interfaces will have progressed to the point of a greater-than-human intelligence that will radically change civilization, and perhaps even human nature.

Technology – the collection of tools, including machinery, modifications, arrangements and procedures used by humans, defined by Kevin Kelly as anything the mind produces.

Technomancy – imaginary or fictional category of magical abilities that affect technology. Also, magical powers gained through the use of technology.

Techosexuals – devotees of robot fetishism.

Transgenic – the process when genetic material from an unrelated organism is added to the host organism.

Transhumanism from Version 2.1 of *The Transhumanist FAQ* – viewed as an extension of humanism, from which it is partially derived. Transhumanist's emphasize that while humans and individuals' matter, that by promoting rational thinking and rational means the human organism can be improved. They argue that technological means can be used beyond traditional humanistic methods to eventually enable humans to move beyond what some would think of as "human."

Transhumanism, alternative – An ideology and movement that affirms the possibility and desirability of improving the human condition by overcoming fundamental human limitations that seek to guide us to a posthumanity condition.

Transhumanist – someone who advocates transhumanism.

Transhuman – intermediary form between the human and posthuman.

Triumvirate – In the past, referred to a group of three men responsible for public administration or civil authority. In the present, a triumvirate refers to a group of people representing three instruments of power: the technocracy, the plutocracy, and our national level government that while not a cabal, and not coordinated, collectively have the power to decide on superintelligence and radical humanoidization that can cause serious disruption to humankind, as we know it.

Turing test – a test performed to determine a machine's ability to exhibit intelligent behavior. The basic concept behind the test is that if a human judge is engaged in a natural language conversation with a computer where he cannot reliably distinguish machine from human, the machine passes the test.

Virtual reality – a simulated environment that your senses perceive as real.

Whole brain emulation (WBE) – Mind upload or brain upload (sometimes called "mind copying" or "mind transfer") is the hypothetical process of scanning the mental state (including long-term memory and "self") of a particular brain substrate and copying it to a computer. The computer could then run a simulation model of the brain's information processing. Then it responds in essentially the same way as the original brain (i.e., indistinguishable from the brain for all relevant purposes) and experiences having a conscious mind.

World Transhumanist Association (WTA) – founded in 1998 and focused on recognition of transhumanism as a legitimate subject of scientific inquiry and public policy. The WTA changed its name to "Humanity+" in 2008 as part of a rebranding to project a more favorable humane image. It launched H+ Magazine and in 2010, the magazine transitioned into a web-only publication.

Xenotransplantation – the process of removing living cells, tissues, or organs from one species and implanting the living cells, tissues, or organs in another species.

Author Bio

James R. Simpson is Affiliate Professor and Senior Fellow, Thomas S. Foley Institute for Public Policy and Public Service, Washington State University, Professor Emeritus, University of Florida, and Professor Emeritus, Ryukoku University, in Japan. His specialty as an international economist includes training and a career as a scientist in techniques and technologies that fit in robotics and artificial intelligence. He has focused on long-term projections of technological change as part of living and working abroad and has engaged in extensive consulting with organizations such as The World Bank. Publications include over 375 articles, monographs and software, and nine books. One of those, that has many hallmarks of the topics in this book, *Is Today's Food Situation Good for Japan? Warning from an American Researcher*, was awarded *Best Book of the Year* by the Japanese Agricultural Journalists Association.